The New Afrikan Blueprints

The New Afrikan Blueprints

Establishing Our Communities Independent of the Government

Abdul Olugbala Shakur
Joka Heshima Jinsai

Additional publications by:

Abdul Olugbala Shakur
Criminology 101: Afrikan Amerikan Politics
Black Guerrilla Diary: Selected Revolutionary Poems
The "Holy Crossword" Puzzle: Biblical Inspired Puzzle
The Afrikan-Amerikan Community Emergency Response Network Manual
Concrete & Steel Center of Excellence: Pan-Afrikan Global Commission against Hunger
Free Speech: Myth or Reality

Abdul Olugbala Shakur & Joka Heshima Jinsai
Poverty Crime and Government: How Amerikkka Criminalized a Race: New Afrikan Criminology 100
Concrete Scholars: Selected Writings Volume I
Abolish Legal Slavery to Prevent Suicide

Joka Heshima Jinsai
Fine Art America (under Shannon Denham Art)
https://fineartamerica.com/art/shannon+denham

For more information contact:

Abdul Olugbala Shakur
James Harvey
C-48884/B-2-128
Kern Valley State Prison
P.O. Box 5102
Delano, CA 93216
abdulolugbalashakur@yahoo.com

Joka Heshima Jinsai
Shannon Lamar Denham
J-38283/B-2-128
P.O. Box 5102
Delano, CA 93216
Kern Valley State Prison
blackstarart276@gmail.com

Table of Contents

Assata Alert Network AAN 1-10
  Abdul Olugbala Shakur

The Afrikan-Amerikan Community Emergency Response
Network 11-27
  Abdul Olugbala Shakur

Concrete and Steel Center of Excellence Pan-Afrikan
Global Commission Against Hunger 28-50
  Abdul Olugbala Shakur

Marcus Garvey Study Group 51-60
  Abdul Olugbala Shakur

Strategic Early Release Program Proposed Proposition 2022 61-65
  Abdul Olugbala Shakur

Operation Hip Hop Rescue: "A Movement" 66-79
  Abdul Olugbala Shakur

A Petition for Institutional Restitution 80-84
  Abdul Olugbala Shakur & Joka Heshima Jinsai

The New Afrikan Security Protocol Mandate 85-107
  Abdul Olugbala Shakur

The Community Safe-Zones Initiative 108-112
  Joka Heshima Jinsai

How to Start a Sustainable Agricultural Commune (S.A.C.)
with the Community 113-114
  Joka Heshima Jinsai

New Afrikan Math & Science Center Initiative 115-123
  Joka Heshima Jinsai

Youth Community Action Program 125-126
  Joka Heshima Jinsai

A BLUE-PRINT TOWARDS BUILDING
SELF-SUFFICIENT COMMUNITIES
TOWARDS BUILDING A NEW AFRIKAN
-NATION-
Abdul Olugbala Shakur
Joka Heshima Jinsai

AAN
WE WILL DO
IT FOR ALL
OF OUR
MISSING
AND GONE
ASSATA ALERT NETWORK
Taking Control
of our
Community Safety
for our
Children,
Women,
&
Elders
AAN

The Assata Alert Network–AAN

MISSION STATEMENT

Rapid loss of protection from internal and external threats due to our inability to provide protection to the children, women, and elders of our communities is the impetus behind the Assata Alert Network. AAN has made it their mission to construct a secured environment dependent on its own community members to protect and defend our children, women, and elders.

Our communities depend on a government that seeks to incarcerate our people, especially our children, rather than educate them. They build more prisons instead of new schools and employ more police officers to patrol our communities, allowing for additional and repeated terroristic trauma to be inflicted upon our people. AAN will never collaborate with the government or law enforcement. We *will* take control of our own communities.

AAN is a national collective network of individuals, groups, communities and organizations who maintain heightened readiness for the prevention and recovery of our missing community members through safety, prevention, education, active patrols, and established safe places.

AAN City Based Committee Members
Chief Coordinator
Deputy Coordinator
Secretary
Treasurer
Chief of Personnel
Security Consultant
Strategist
Chief Researcher

Note: A brief description for each AAN City-Based Committee Member position will be provided upon request. Changes are allowed by each city chapter as they deem necessary.

AAN MANIFESTO

The nature of our stated mission has influenced the construct of our functional infrastructure; we are a community based security network serving in the interest of our communities. We as a People/Community face the rapid loss to protect our own children, women, and elders from both internal and external threats.

Our inability and failure to secure our communities due to a lack of our own security plays a large role in the increased frequency of abduction, rape, molestation, and murder of our children. Our Elders live in fear of leaving their homes, and our women, whether prostitutes or college students, are increasingly becoming victims of abuse, serial rapists, and serial killers. Outsiders who own local liquor stores, grocery markets, laundromats, and landlords, along with law enforcement disrespect our communities and abuse our children, women and elders. While it is understandable our People are frustrated and live in fear, those emotions only impair one's vision to see the reality and truth of the situation. The majority of our People tend to equate a secured Community with government/law enforcement. This is a grave error. Law enforcement cannot be our source of protection; rather, it is the cause of great harm and racial injustices to our communities.

Defining a Secured Community

The definition of a secured community is one with the ability and capacity of determination to protect its members from any threats. Therefore, protecting our communities as a community based security network means:

1. Protecting our children with our own ability and capacity of determination from abuse, violence, rape, molestation, abduction and abandonment.
2. Protecting our women with our own ability and capacity of determination from violence, rape, abuse, abduction, prostitution, and erotic entertainment/exploitation.

3. Protecting our elders with our own ability and capacity of determination from abuse, violence, crime/fraud and exploitation.
4. Protecting our communities with our own ability and capacity of determination from all internal and or external threats.

Prevention vs Reaction

AAN's goal is to construct a secured environment, allowing fulfillment of their mission to protect and defend our children, women and elders; primarily focusing on locating our missing children, women and elders.

Reactive approaches have repeatedly fallen in line with the old familiar quote, "doing the same thing over and over and expecting different results." While there are numerous groups from all races of people and affiliations committed to locating missing children, women and elders, over 64,000 remain unfound, which reflects reactive measures are failing our people. It is obvious preventive measures must be taken before abductions or economic struggles occur. For example: if a mother is working as an exotic dancer to provide for her children and pay for college tuition, preventive measures have not been considered. What we need to learn from this is if you want different outcomes, you must try different strategies.

AAN endeavors to do things *different,* and their primary strategy within their mission will be to take control of their own community security. In line with AAN's mission statement, prevention also involves a secure environment, allowing to effectively educate our community on employing the proper methods needed to avoid and prevent the abductions, rape/molestation and murder of our children, women and elders. When a community lacks a *sense* of community, especially as it pertains to security, it creates an open door environment for predators to prey upon our children, women and elders. Thus the focus of AAN is on prevention, requiring additional systems to be established within our communities such as:

- Educational institutions independent of a government who historically has not valued the educational, physical, mental or emotional lives of our children.
- Resources and provisions including, but not limited to food, housing for homeless, employment, and physical, mental, or emotional care of our children, women and elders.

AAN RESPONSIBILITIES AND FUNCTIONS

Our communities have depended on a government that seeks to incarcerate our people, especially our children, rather than educate them. They build more prisons instead of new schools, and employ more police officers to patrol our communities, allowing for additional and repeated terroristic trauma to be inflicted upon our people. AAN will never collaborate with the government or law enforcement. We *will* take control of our own community.

With the primary function of AAN being on prevention, our process begins with ensuring our children, women and elders have a safe and secure environment to live their lives free from abduction, abuse, and/or murder. Creating such an environment will be the responsibility of *all* AAN personnel.

AAN INITIATIVES: STANDARD COMMUNITY ORGANIZATION INITIATIVES

(Initiatives will be included as addendums)

These methods will be incorporated to carry out our programs at ground zero by implementing two (2) Standard Community Organization Initiatives.

The New Afrikan Community Security Protocol Mandate (NASPM)

The NASPM manual, by founder Khalid Shakur, calls for AAN personnel and volunteers, in conjunction with the Community, to build the basic infrastructure to ensure our Communities of children, women and elders are defended from the following internal and external threats (not to be considered an all-inclusive list of threats):

- Violence
- Abuse
- Abduction
- Criminality
- Fraud
- Exploitation
- Discrimination

❖ The aforementioned list *will* be accomplished *without* aid or involvement of government or law enforcement.

Community Safe Zones Initiative

The Community Safe Zones Initiative, drafted by Joka Heshima Jinsai, calls for us to garrison the spaces in our Communities most frequented by our children, women, and elders to ensure our People can engage in daily life without fear if abduction, abuse or violent death. The initiative is site based, and will require constant communication and volunteer participation to both identify those sites designated to be safe zones, and deploying volunteers to garrison those sites in teams of two (2).

An additional component of this initiative requires engaging sub-culture elements (i.e., gang members, etc.) to ensure they are aware of and respect the safe zones. Gang members have young siblings, mothers, children and elders, and will – if engaged – support any Community based initiative in an effort to keep their loved ones safe.

THE 7 PRINCIPLES

The foundation of the Standard Community Organization Initiative and the Community Safe Zones Initiative is rooted in the Nguzo Saba, or "The 7 Principles." This provides the appropriate psychological and cultural source for all our activities on behalf of our children, women, and elders. Each member of AAN will familiarize themselves with "The 7 Principles" and to the best of their ability practice them in their daily lives.

The 7 Principles

- **Unity**: To strive for and maintain unity in the family, community, nation and race.

- **Collective Work and Responsibility**: To build and maintain our community together and make our brother's and sister's problems our problems and to solve them together.
- **Cooperative Economics**: To build and maintain our own stores, shops and other businesses and to profit from them together.
  - **Self-Determination**: To define ourselves, name ourselves, create for ourselves and speak for ourselves.
- **Purpose**: To make building and developing of our community our collective vocation to restore our people to their traditional greatness.
  - **Creativity**: To do always as much as we can, in the way we can, to leave our community more beautiful and beneficial than we inherited it.
  - **Faith**: To believe with all our heart in our people, our parents, our teachers, our leaders and the righteousness and victory of our struggle.

To ensure the successful implementation of both initiatives into our communities at a local, state, and regional level, the overall AAN programs must be structured at ground zero. To accomplish this, for each community we will organize a local AAN Coordinating Committee. These committees will oversee the performance of the AAN work and initiatives. The composition of the AAN Coordinating Committee's will be outlined in the section on STRUCTURE.

AAN Personnel Guidelines

All AAN personnel will function within the basic guidelines outlined as **All AAN personnel**:

- Are to be vigilant and watchful at all times in and around our Communities to identify, neutralize or eliminate any internal and external threats to our children, women and elders.
- Will be trained in assertiveness and communication skills to effectively communicate to and with members of the Community.

- Will be trained in basic self-defense, to include Tasers, pepper spray and small arms.
- Will be trained in basic search and rescue techniques (i.e. grid searching, online searches, observation of details, basic tracking, CPR, etc.).
- Will know their neighbors and many members of their Community, as well as being intimately familiar with the physical structure of their Community itself and the surrounding area.

AAN Protocols

1. The AAN under no circumstances will work with the government and/or law enforcement. Violation of this protocol will result in the immediate expulsion of the individual and or group
2. The AAN will not accept any grants or funds from any government agencies or entities. Violation of this protocol will result in the immediate expulsion of the involved.
3. Hostility is unacceptable in AAN; our mission is clear. Identify the parties involved and put them on probation, if anyone repeats this act, they will be expelled.

Note: Each AAN City-Based chapter can implement their own additional rules and protocols, but the above three can never be removed. Any AAN City-Based chapter that attempts to remove them will be immediately expelled.

While AAN is a Black Movement/Formation managed solely by Black people, members of other races are welcome to assist us.

AAN Teams

AAN necessities these teams:

    A) Search Team
    B) Research Team
    C) Security Team
    D) Patrol Team

Every City-Based AAN chapter must establish a line of communication with all City Based AAN chapters in their state. The Chief Coordinator of every City-Based AAN chapter will prepare an oversight committee to ensure that every City-Based AAN chapter is functioning according to our Manifesto

Non-Lethal Self-Defense Weapons

Many of our women, children and elders are increasingly becoming victims of abuse, serial rapists, sex trafficking, and serial killers. There are numerous weapons for self-defense that are non-lethal. These deliver enough protection to keep our sistas, children and elders safe but not powerful enough to cause any fatalities.

Mixed martial arts:
Turning your body into your own weapon is a MUST. Most attackers look for "easy targets", not People who are ready and willing to defend themselves. Knowing basic Martial Art skills can be enough to disarm and discourage an attacker.

Pepper Spray:
Pepper Spray is a potent but non-lethal weapon for self-defense by targeting the predator's eyesight. It is effective at giving our women, children and elders several minutes to defend themselves or flee from the attacker.

Tasers:
Tasers are considered the *king* of non-lethal weapons. Tasers occasionally are linked to death, but this occurs when the attackers fall down after being tased and hit their head or if they have health conditions. Before using any non-lethal weapon, you *must* learn the proper use and training to operate it correctly. Before purchasing non-lethal weapons such as Tasers, check if you can carry/operate one in your state.

Tactical flashlight:
Tactical Flashlights are bright and small; easy to carry. Shining them into an attacker's eyes could be enough to briefly stun them, which could give you a few seconds to flee or defend yourself.

Mini stun gun with security alarm:
A stun gun is a close contact weapon that requires you to hold the weapon close to your attacker's body to deliver a shock. It delivers a powerful jolt of electricity that courses through the attacker's body.

Self Defense knives:
A Self Defense Knife requires you to get close to your attacker, making you more vulnerable and can give them the opportunity to take your weapon. Use a self-defense knife if you are in a dire situation and your life is on the line. Like most other weapons on this list, you *must* learn the proper way to use self-defense knives and be trained correctly.

Batons:
In the case of an attack, you can use a Baton to defend yourself against an aggressor by hitting them in the arms, legs, hands or collarbone. A baton is a great non-lethal weapon to keep in your home and any other place in case of emergency because there are no directions or lessons needed to use it.

The Afrikan-Amerikan Community Emergency Response Network Manual

Presented by

Concrete & Steel Center of Excellence

Abdul Olugbala Shakur

aka James E. Harvey

The Afrikan-Amerikan Community Emergency Response Network Manual

Preamble

Unfortunately, many within the Afrikan-Amerikan (aka New Afrikan) community don't take natural disasters or crises seriously, and our community's failure to prepare itself for a natural disaster is indicative of that criticism. We are approximately eleven (11) years removed from Hurricane Katrina, and not one Afrikan-Amerikan community has effectively or independently prepared itself in light of the tragedy. We can no longer afford to depend on the government or any outside sources; our vulnerability becomes more fragile when we depend on outsiders or others to do for us what we can do for ourselves. Developing our own emergency network and/or manual is no longer an option; it is now a necessity towards the survival of our People/community. The key to surviving a natural disaster, or at least minimizing fatalities, is being prepared and organized. This emergency response manual is only a blue-print in the service of our communities. It contains two (2) inter-connecting components:

1. A plan for the individual family.
2. A more complex and long-range plan designed to prepare our communities.

Abdul Olugbala Shakur
aka James E. Harvey

Home Preparation and Survival

Many of our people are unprepared for natural disasters or a major crisis, and often, attempt to prepare themselves at the last minute when food and/or emergency supplies at most stores are almost depleted, and then they compete for limited supplies, or loot to obtain their basic necessities to survive. This is not how you prepare yourself or your family. To the contrary, this is a last minute act of desperation. No disrespect intended, but this is not a smart decision making process. For the most part, we as a People do not think strategically or tactically, and this is one of our major obstacles towards solving our day-to-day problems and moving forward as a People. I ask, *Why would you wait until the last minute to prepare yourself or your family? Especially when you know every year there exists the potential for a natural disaster or major crisis. Do you value your safety and that of your family? Because, if you do, your action/response(s) are not indicative of such values.*

We must take this issue more seriously than we are, **<u>NOT WHEN THE DISASTER OR CRISIS IS AT OUR FRONT DOOR.</u>** I equally understand that most Afrikan-Amerikan families don't know what to do, nor do they have access to the information that would empower them with the capacity to effectively prepare themselves. So as a direct result, we developed this comprehensive emergency response manual, a blueprint towards constructing a community-based emergency response network. The first step towards achieving this goal is to prepare every family/household in our community. Once this is established, this would serve as the foundation for the development and implementation of our community emergency network operation.

<u>Home Preparation</u>

Each household must develop an emergency plan based on the natural disasters common in their area. Each natural disaster will determine how one responds and/or prepares. Preparing for an earthquake differs from preparing for a hurricane, though the supplies that are required in facilitating our preparation are similar, if not the same. It is imperative for one's survival to clearly identify all the disasters you are annually subjected to and organize accordingly.

There exist three (3) primary components that complement an effective emergency response plan:
1. An emergency plan.
2. Home survival kit.
3. Bug-Out-Bag(s).

<u>**An emergency plan**</u>: The first step in surviving a natural disaster and/or crisis is having a practical and comprehensive plan. It doesn't

have to be elaborate or complicated. Keep it simple. The unfortunate reality is Hurricane Katrina was and is our learning curve. It taught us what not to do and what we must do to survive a natural disaster. Most of our People/community in New Orleans did not have a plan, and as a direct result many suffered more than what they had to. An emergency response plan would have dramatically mitigated the unnecessary suffering.

The basic emergency plan should at the very least consist of:

1. **<u>An Evacuation Plan</u>**: You and your family should conduct emergency drills at least once or twice a month. Each family member must learn how to evacuate. If you live in an apartment building or housing project, the evacuation becomes a little more complicated and urgent; you cannot afford to wait until the last minute to evacuate. If you live in an apartment building or housing project, you need to purchase a rope-ladder(s), or long-ladders, if possible from an economic stand point, if not, you and your neighbors should pool your money together and purchase these items that will serve all that are affected. The rope-ladders must be strategically located.
   *Note: To ensure success, we insist that you seek training from an expert on how to install and use the rope-ladders/and long-ladders. Often during certain emergency evacuations family members are separated, so it becomes critical that each family (if possible) designate a specific location to meet or call, from a relative's house to your Mosque/Church, or even an emergency relief center. Each family should also develop their own identification (ID) card; this ID card will have the basic info, such as name, multiple contact numbers, and medical information if applicable. This would help emergency relief workers to reunite family members, and/or identify dead bodies.

I reiterate: identify your specific disaster zone(s), such as floods, earthquakes, wildfires, snowstorms, etc. Your emergency plan must be based on the specific disaster(s) in your area/community. Adding routes to avoid with heavy traffic should also be added to your evacuation plan. Studying every route in your community/area is important in developing the most effective evacuation emergency plan.

B) <u>**Home Survival Kit**</u>:
1. Bottled water; don't pay for bottled water, bottle your own water before the natural disaster/or crisis affects the drinking water.
2. Non-perishable food items.
3. Faraday flashlights.
4. Old Brooklyn Lanterns.
5. Insta light emergency bulbs.
6. Flints.
7. Matches/Waterproof Matches.
8. Flares.
9. Battery-Operated Radios.
10. Cell-phones/Disposal cell-phones (if affordable).
11. Compass(es).
12. Lap-top Computers.
13. Portable Fire Extinguisher(s).
14. Portable Generator: Don't use generator(s) indoors.
15. Space bags: These bags are good for putting your clothes in, along with other valuables, such as family photos, and important documents; and have your contact information either inside the bag, or attached to the outside, whatever method(s) is most effective.
16. Ladder/Rope.
17. Shovel/Short-hand shovel(s).
18. Axe/Hatchet.
19. Hacksaw/Hacksaw Blades.
20. Gloves.
21. Sleeping Bag(s).
22. Ziploc Bags.
23. Water Purification Kit/System.
24. Weapons to defend your home and/or family such as:
    - Guns
    - Crossbows
    - Knives
    - Tasers

- Pepper Spray(s)
25. Life-Jackets/Life-Rafts (if applicable for flood-zones).
26. Whistles and clickers, these items help emergency workers locate you, if you cannot blow your whistles; the clickers can be as effective.
27. First Aid Kit: The Home-based first aid kit will differ from the mobile/carried first aid kits; space is not that much of an issue, allowing one to stock more medical supplies, but the basics will still be required. We also insist that every family take a basic first aid course.

C) **<u>Bug-Out-Bag</u>**: some emergencies will require that you and your family leave the house/or shelter, and often many of our people rush out of their homes empty handed and unprepared for the emergency about to confront them. A Bug-Out-Bag is a back pack that contains all the basic necessities that one keeps *on the ready*. When a natural disaster hits and it's time to evacuate, everything you and/or your family will need should be in your Bug-Out-Bag; if you have a family, you should have at least two to three additional Bug-Out-Bags. (e.g. depending on how many family members you will be responsible for). Besides your primary Bug-Out-Bag, each family member should wear a survival parka shell. These waterproof jackets have multiple pockets providing additional space to carry more emergency supplies.

Your Bug-Out-Bag should consist of these items:
1. A pair of thick thermal underwear (top and bottom).
2. A liner and outer socks.
3. Rugged Gloves.
4. Battery-Operated Radios.
5. Lap-top Computer(s)/Cell-phones(s).
6. Compass/GPS.
7. Water filter system/water purification tablets.
8. Water Bladder (e.g. MRS Platypus 2-Liter).
9. Sleeping Bag(s)/Life-Jackets/Life-Preservers.
10. Flash lights/extra batteries, and LED Headlamp(s).
11. Fire starter-Butane lighter/Flint/Waterproof Matches.
12. Folding Multiple-function tool/knife(s).
13. Legal and Registered Gun(s).
14. Whistle(s)/clicker(s).

15. Cup/Spoon/fork(s).
16. Nonperishable food: e.g. Nuts, Dry Fruits, Rice, Chocolate, Raisins, Granola Bars, Trail Mix.
17. First Aid Kit.

Your first aid kit should consist of:
a) A couple of pairs of nitrile gloves.
b) Two tubes of antibiotic ointment.
c) Rolls of one-inch wide safety tape/Butterfly sutures in various sizes.
d) Two sterile suture kits.
e) Two Bottles Ibuprofen.
f) At least three thermometers.
g) 25 Alcohol prep-pads.
h) Three tubes of liquid hand soap.
i) 1 or 2 Bottles of Multi-vitamins.
j) Loperamide Hydrochloride Anti-diarrhea caplets.
k) Katadyn Micropur MP1 water purification tablets.
l) Three packages of glucose tablets (for hypoglycemia).
m) One pair of EMS shears.
n) Two lock forceps.
o) Two small pair scissors.
p) One pair of toenail clippers.
q) One pair of tweezers.
r) 20 quick-clot antimicrobial hemostatic pack, 50gm (stop bleeding fast).
s) Two packages of sewing needles in various sizes.
t) One small flash light/headlamp(s).

Note: We suggest that you pick up a copy of the U.S. Army first aid manual. Also check out these sites:

www.redcrossstore.org
www.quickclot.com
www.foodsmart.gov.
www.niosh.gov

Afrikan-Amerikan Community Emergency Response Network

We will avoid bureaucratic stagnation, so instead of establishing one central agency, every state will have its own Afrikan-Amerikan

Community Emergency Response Network (A.A.C.E.R.N.). This network will prepare every Afrikan-Amerikan (aka New Afrikan) community in their state (i.e. jurisdiction) for a natural disaster/crisis. This network will be elected/selected by our communities. We will develop a state-wide ballot system that would allow our People/Community to vote. Only those who live in the New Afrikan community will be eligible to sit on the Board of Directors (A.A.C.E.R.N.), and they must be well known community-activists with a history of serving our community. The community will have the power to remove any Board member they are dissatisfied with. The A.A.C.E.R.N. will work with the **Amerikan-Red Cross**, and other emergency services, but we will not be subordinate to them, nor will we be dictated to or serve as a government puppet.

The A.A.C.E.R.N. will consist of:
1. Director
2. Director of Expropriation
3. 3 additional Board Members
4. Deputy Director
5. Director of Information
6. Treasurer
7. Emergency Evacuation Chief Coordinator
8. Secretary
9. Chief Medical Advisor
10. Chief Security Coordinator
11. Chief Meteorologist
12. Logistic Management Coordinator

Emergency Response Committee

Every city with New Afrikan communities will be eligible to form an Emergency Response Committee (E.R.C.). The same rules that apply to the A.A.C.E.R.N. also apply to the E.R.C.; every E.R.C. member will be elected/selected by the Afrikan-Amerikan community in that city. They will be known community-activists with no affiliation with the government or law enforcement. The People will also have the power to remove any member from the E.R.C. they are dissatisfied with. **ALL** E.R.C. are accountable to the state-based A.A.C.E.R.N. in their state.

Each E.R.C. must file a monthly report to the state-based A.A.C.E.R.N., the E.R.C. status report will basically consist of all relevant information pertaining to their stated purpose, mission/goals, progresses, failures, and most important, a financial report. This is a brief example. The E.R.C. will be ultimately responsible for implementing this blue-print; the E.R.C. will also have community level representatives.

The E.R.C. will consist of:
1. Executive Coordinator
2. Expropriation Coordinator
3. Deputy Coordinator
4. Emergency Evacuation Coordinator
5. Treasurer
6. Information Coordinator
7. Secretary
8. Deputy Medical Advisor
9. Security Coordinator
10. Deputy Meteorologist
11. Logistic Coordinator
12. Three additional Board Members

Emergency Response Services
1. Emergency Survey Unit (E.S.U.).
2. Emergency Mobile Clinics (E.M.C.).
3. Emergency Ambulance Services (E.A.S.).
4. Emergency Medical Stations (E.M.S.).
5. Emergency Medical Staff Assistance (E.M.S.A.).
6. Emergency Evacuation Unit (E.E.U.).
7. Emergency Expropriation Network (E.E.N.).
8. Emergency Security Network (E.S.N.).
9. Emergency Information Center (E.I.C.).
10. Emergency Food and Water Services (E.F.W.S.).
11. Emergency Logistic Management Network (E.L.M.N.).
12. Emergency Mobile Safety Deposit Box (E.M.S.D.B.).
13. Community Emergency Trust Fund (C.E.T.F.).

Emergency Survey Unit

The E.S.U. will be activated before, during and after a natural disaster. The E.S.U. will monitor all the local dams, levees, flood walls/gates. They will also search for structural damages in all the local housing projects, apartments, schools, bridges, freeway overpasses. The E.S.U. will conduct monthly tests of all drinking water; especially during and after a crisis/natural disaster. The E.S.U. will also identify all Afrikan-Amerikan communities/areas prone to floods, earthquakes, hurricanes, tornados, snow and tropical storms, and bush/wild fires. This unit will file a report every 90 days detailing their findings. A copy of this report will be sent to the state-based A.A.C.E.R.N., the city-based E.R.C. and the designated emergency response services. The A.A.C.E.R.N. in that state will share this report with the community, local and state emergency services.

Emergency Mobile Clinics

During Hurricane Katrina many of our people could not reach a hospital or receive emergency medical attention, and as a direct result, many suffered, if not died. The E.M.C. will be fully equipped, and capable of performing certain emergency operations and/or procedures, which will include X-rays. The E.M.C. will be dispatched to the hardest hit areas, especially those in rural areas. We will also send an E.M.C. to all the emergency relief centers and evacuee shelters. We will also have Emergency Mobile Boat Clinics which would allow us to reach our people in the flooded areas.

Emergency Ambulance Services

We will convert old/new vans and boats into fully equipped ambulances. The E.A.S. will be activated/and active all year round, but during a crisis/natural disaster their priority will be to:

1. Reach the most vulnerable.
2. To transport the injured to the Emergency Medical Station (E.M.S.), Emergency Mobile Clinics (E.M.C.), and when applicable, to the local hospitals not damaged by the crisis/natural disaster.

<u>**Note**</u>: The E.A.S. will also develop its own emergency dispatch system.

<u>Emergency Medical Station</u>

The E.M.S. are temporary make-shift hospitals (i.e. triages). During Hurricane Katrina many of the local hospitals were damaged, if not seriously affected by the flood water, and there were those that were just too far away. We will establish fully equipped E.M.S. in areas designated safe/secured. We will also set up E.M.S. at designated emergency relief centers and evacuee shelters.

<u>Emergency Medical Staff Assistance</u>

The E.M.S.A. are our first responders. They will be trained in first aid and other advanced medical treatment. We will have at least three (3) E.M.S.A. on every block. They will be responsible for the People on their block.

Their responsibility will consist of:

1. Teaching everyone on their block first aid.
2. Providing every house on their block with a first aid kit.
3. Teach everyone on their block how to swim. Identifying all the most vulnerable on their block, such as the handicapped, elders, children and the sick.
4. Develop a data-base of all those who live on their block who suffer from some type of health problems. This data-base will describe the health problem(s), and provide a list of the medication they are taking, and the name of their doctor/health-care provider(s).
5. Develop emergency medical bracelets for those listed in their data base. This would allow emergency medical workers access to their medical data during a crisis/natural disaster. We will develop a computer program designed to secure this data against theft.

<u>Emergency Evacuation Unit</u>

During Hurricane Katrina many of our people died because they did not have the means or know how to evacuate, or the evacuation was not properly organized.

The E.E.U. will be responsible for:
1. Developing an effective evacuation plan for the community.
2. Coordinating the evacuation of the community.
3. **<u>Conducting evacuation drills at least two to three times a year, more if applicable.</u>**
4. Developing an evacuation emergency plan manual, and distribute copies to our communities.
5. Establishing a working relationship with the school district that would allow them to utilize all available school buses to evacuate the people. The E.E.U. will also have a The Afrikan-Amerikan Community Emergency Response Network Manual.
6. The number of boats in their services.
      <u>Note</u>: Children, elders, the sick and women will be priority.

<u>Emergency Expropriation Network</u>

We do not agree with the government position on looting during a crisis/natural disaster. We also equally disagree with looting as an effective means towards obtaining sustenance for human survival during a crisis/natural disaster. We have a more effective method to achieve this objective. During a crisis/natural disaster the E.E.N. will dispatch a unit to all the affected grocery, hardware and clothing stores along with a unit from our Emergency Security Network (E.S.N.) to secure these businesses while the E.E.N. expropriate the necessary supplies.

The E.E.N. will focus on the following supplies:
1. All food items, including baby food and candy.
2. Bottled water, milk, juice and sodas.

3. Coats, rain coats, sweat shirts/pants, thermal tops/bottoms, socks, gloves, wool bennies, boots, blankets, sleeping bags, space bags, towels.
4. Matches, waterproof matches, flints, lighters, flash lights, lanterns, flares, batteries.
5. Paper cups/plates, plastic forks/spoons, toilet paper, paper towels, pampers, tampons, zip-lock bags, garbage bags, cooking pots/pans.
6. Barbeque grills, charcoal, portable fire extinguishers, portable generators, battery-operated radios.
7. Ropes, rope ladders, ladders, hammers, hacksaws, hacksaw blades, saws, hatchets, axes, shovels, shorthand shovels, screw drivers, socket wrench set, water hoses, wheelbarrow, tents, life-rafts, life jackets, chainsaws.
8. The Emergency Logistic Management Network (E.L.M.N.) will coordinate the distribution of the above supplies to those in need. The E.E.N. will inventory each item expropriated by the E.E.N. in the service of the People, and provide copies to all those business owners affected by our survival expropriation. This will minimize unnecessary looting.

<u>Emergency Security Network</u>

THE E.S.N. will have two (2) different divisions:
1. An Armed Division.
2. An Unarmed Division.

The E.S.N. will be a legitimate community-based security network, **<u>no cops, paid informants or puppets for law enforcement</u>**. The E.S.N. will be a community-based controlled and licensed network activated during a crisis/natural disaster. Unfortunately, there was some truth to the report that at least a few young men used Hurricane Katrina as an opportunity to victimize their own People, **<u>but so-called law enforcement also used Hurricane Katrina as an opportunity to murder some of our young men, as their own record would reflect.</u>** We will dispatch units from our E.S.N. to secure our communities, children, women, elders and our evacuee-shelters/relief centers.

Note: The unarmed divisions will have The Afrikan-Amerikan Community Emergency Response Network Manual to assist the Emergency Evacuation Unit in evacuating the people and other designated areas of responsibilities.

Emergency Information Center

One of the principal elements inherent to effective preparation is information. Accurate information facilitates a community's endeavors to prepare itself for a crisis/natural disaster. One of our primary weaknesses is not having enough information, or the infrastructure to process and distribute vital information to our people/Community.

The E.I.C. will be responsible for:

1. Developing an emergency survival manual.
   This manual will contain all the information on what to do during specific crises/natural disasters. For example: though there are basic similarities — each natural force has its own distinctive characteristics that call for a specific response. This manual will have an emergency response plan for each natural force (e.g. Tornados, Floods, Earthquakes, Hurricanes, wildfires, to name a few).

2. The E.I.C. will develop an emergency response directory listing the addresses, phone numbers, websites and e-mails of all our emergency response services listed in our manual, including all state-based A.A.C.E.R.N. and city-based E.R.C. in the country.

3. During Hurricane Katrina many of our families were separated and our children lost. The E.I.C. will develop an Afrikan-Amerikan (i.e. New Afrikan) family central data-base. Every city-based E.I.C. will develop an Afrikan-Amerikan central data-base containing all Afrikan-Amerikans in their city. For example: Let's say we have the Shakur's family, the data-base will list all family members and relatives, and the pictures of the immediate family members (this is optional and a decision reserved for each family). This option will be

available to all New Afrikan families in our E.I.C. data-base. Each family will have their own personal emergency instructions, instructing their individual family members what to do, where to go and who to contact. Each family will have their own personal and secured access code to their specific page on our data-base.

This would provide emergency workers access to vital information to re-unite lost loved ones. It would also allow emergency workers to immediately identify lost children or even dead bodies.

4. It will also be the responsibility of the E.I.C. to develop an emergency communication network that would allow all our emergency services/workers to communicate with one another during a crisis/natural disaster. The E.I.C. must develop their own dispatch system.

The E.I.C. is one of the most vital components in the success of an independent Afrikan-Amerikan (i.e. New Afrikan) controlled emergency response network. Note: High-tech will play a major role in this endeavor.

Emergency Food and Water Services

During Hurricane Katrina many of our people went three to six days without food or water. The E.F.W.S. will establish emergency food and water banks distributed during a crisis/natural disaster. During natural disasters the E.F.W.S. will establish emergency food and water stations in unaffected areas, as well as relief centers and evacuee shelters. The Afrikan-Amerikan Community Emergency Response Network Manual E.F.W.S. will also have mobile kitchens that will distribute food and water to families trapped in affected areas.

Emergency Logistic Management Network

The E.L.M.N. will be a multi-task network, for it will work closely with all the Emergency Response Services listed in this manual. The E.L.M.N. will ensure that all Afrikan-Amerikan (New Afrikan) emergency services are equipped, adequately supplied and functional. They will also establish and maintain several stock-piles of emergency supplies throughout their jurisdiction in areas designated by the Emergency Survey Unit (E.S.U.)

The E.L.M.N. inventory will consist of:
1. Medical equipment/Supplies and first aid kit.
2. Bottled water.
3. Non-perishable food.
4. Coats, rain coats, boots, wool bennies, thermal shirts and pants, sweat shirts and pants, socks and gloves.
5. Matches/waterproof matches, flints, flares, fire-wicks, butane lighters, flash lights, old Brooklyn lanterns, Insta bulbs, batteries.
6. Blankets, sleeping bags, tents, life-rafts, life-jackets, space bags, towels.
7. Garbage bags, zip lock bags, toilet paper, pampers, tampons, paper plates/cups, plastic forks/spoons, pots and pans, barbecue grills, charcoal.
8. Battery-operated radios, cell-phones, lap-tops computers, portable fire extinguishers, portable generators, water purification systems.
9. Ladders, rope ladders, ropes, hacksaws, hacksaw blades, saws, chainsaws, hammers, screw drivers, shovels, short-hand shovels, socket wrench sets, axes, hatchets, water hose, wheelbarrows.

The E.L.M.N. will also coordinate the distribution of supplies during a crisis/natural disaster. The E.L.M.N. will also make sure that every New Afrikan family is armed with a survival kit, especially those who cannot afford to purchase the necessary supplies.

Emergency Mobile Safety Deposit Box

During most Tornados, Hurricanes, Floods and Wildfires many of our people lose valuable documents, family pictures and other family valuables, such as jewelry. The E.M.S.D.B. will convert trailer trucks into mobile safety deposit boxes. They will have small safe deposit boxes securely mounted on the inside walls of the trucks with locked doors. Each New Afrikan (i.e. Afrikan Amerikan) family that sign up for this service will be assigned a box(s) and given a key. The E.M.S.D.B. will drive throughout the community hours before the potential crisis/natural disaster and allow those families to place their valuables in their secured safety deposit box(s). The E.M.S.D.B. will be driven to a secured safe place/location and guarded by a division of our Emergency Security Network (armed division). The community will always select the drivers and guards of these Mobile Safety Deposit Boxes.

<u>Conclusion</u>

My People, what disturbed me the most about Hurricane Katrina was not the government or law enforcement's failure to help our people/community, it was watching New Afrikan Men Standing around helplessly **(Note: I am aware that many of our Brothas took the initiative to help our People/Community during Hurricane Katrina, but for the most part, we were missing in action)**, while our community, women, children, elders, handicapped and sick suffered. Mostly, our Men did not know what to do, though many tried to help. I don't mean to sound harsh, but if we expect to avoid another Hurricane Katrina, we must conduct a true and honest critique of our failures. But this is an opportunity for us to empower ourselves/community with the capacity and capability to prepare our People/Community for any crisis/natural disaster, without depending on others to do for us what we should do for ourselves. Please understand this manual is not an invitation to become dependent on government or any other outside entity; this manual is a call to stand up for ourselves, and take responsibility for ourselves and of our future.

ABDUL OLUGBALA SHAKUR

CONCRETE & STEEL

Center of Excellence

PAN-AFRIKAN GLOBAL COMMISSION AGAINST HUNGER

August 6, 2020
By *Concrete & Steel Scholar* Abdul Olugbala Shakur

The Pan-Afrikan Global Commission Against Hunger

INTRODUCTION

It has been estimated that one out of eight children in the United States go to bed hungry, which is a deplorable commentary on the human morality in the U.S., especially when we live in the richest country in the world. Hunger is a preventable and does not equate to a Social-Illness and disease. A disease which could be controlled and eventually eradicated, but due to the lack of an effective program, we are forced to depend on a government that does not even give a damn about our New Afrikan/Global Afrikan children and community; a government quick to build new prisons to incarcerate our children. My People, at present we own no means of mass-food production or distribution. Many of our children/people are forced to resort to dehumanizing means just to get food. None of our children, or people for that matter, should be forced to eat out of garbage cans or soup kitchens. Soup kitchens, government-sponsored hand-outs should not become a permanent infrastructure within our communities. The time has come for us as a people and global community to develop our own means to feed our people and community. This proposal was originally written back in 1997, its original title was: "The New Afrikan Community Department of Agriculture," and has been revised twenty (20) times. Many people/community and organizations have only paid lip service to implementing our proposal. We can no longer afford to depend on people and organizations outside of our community to promote or implement this proposal. So from my prison cell, where I've been for the past 34 ½ years, while spending the last 32 years in solitary confinement, I intend to promote and implement this much-needed proposal.

Under this revised proposal, The New Afrikan Community Department of Agriculture will now be called: "Pan-Afrikan Global Commission Against Hunger," and it will have a Pan-Afrikan global function and purpose. Meaning, not only will it serve the needs of our domestic New Afrikan (i.e. Afrikan-Amerikan) community, it is also designed to serve the needs of the entire "Black Diaspora." As I have often written, hunger and starvation are preventable social diseases that the "so-called" developed world (e.g., European countries including Amerikkka and Canada) via Kolonialism/Neo-Kolonialism has precipitated and politically exploited. But, I will not use this proposal as a medium toward identifying blame, because it is now our responsibility to combat and eradicate hunger and starvation among our children and people, not only in the United States, but the entire Black Diaspora, we must establish a foundation and international headquarters. Despite our daily struggle against racial oppression, racism, and violent repression, we as New Afrikans (i.e. Afrikans in Amerikkka) are more stable and better off than all our Brothers/Sisters in the Global Black Diaspora. We have access to more resources and technological skills as it relates to agriculture. Plus, we are more financially stable. These facts make it more applicable for the International Headquarters to be established here in the United States. Under this revised proposal, there will exist two (2) distinct divisions without our proposed Pan-Afrikan Global Commission Against Hunger (PAGCAH): A domestic division and an international division.

Domestic Division

The responsibility of this division is two-fold:

1. To combat and eradicate hunger and starvation in the New Afrikan community within the borders of North Amerika, and

2. To build and establish the foundation/headquarters that would allow the PAGCAH to serve the needs and interest of the Global Black Diaspora.

International Division

The responsibility of this division is more complex and multi-dimensional. Not only will it combat hunger and starvation within our

Black Global Diaspora, but it will be equally responsible for developing an International Banking System specifically for our Global Black Diaspora. This element will serve as a commission on import and export and allow us to exchange much needed goods, such as food items, technology, medical supplies and equipment. This division will also initiate a global movement to restore ownership of all mineral rights back to the original inhabitants of Mother-Afrika. We also intend to initiate the Global Black Diaspora Reparation Trust Fund (GBDRTF); however, the most crucial aspect of this division is the **Council on Infrastructural Development (CID).** There are many countries within the Global Black Diaspora from Haiti to Liberia faced with rapid deteriorating infrastructures and without a stable internal infrastructure we deprive ourselves (i.e. Global Family) of a capacity to effectively help our People feed themselves.

Unlike other efforts to end hunger/starvation we believe in empowering the People with the capacity to feed themselves. The traditional approach is not the answer; it makes the People more dependent on outside forces that politically exploit their suffering. There are also religious groups that use these human crises to force-feed the poor and hungry their religious doctrine, pretending to care under the cloak of Christianity. The goal of the PAGCAH is designed to eradicate hunger/starvation within the Global Black Diaspora and stabilize our Global Black Diaspora (GDB). It has been the goal of the Global White Imperialist Oligarchy (GWIO) to keep us weak, unstable, dependent, and obsolete in world affairs. Implementing this proposal will be a powerful blow against Global White Supremacy. The AGCAH will not be based on the principle of U.S. Kapitalism nor on the principles of Russia/China pseudo socialism. The principle foundation of the PAGCAH is rooted in New Afrikan equalitarianism, which is indigenous to our historical struggle as New Afrikans fighting for liberation and justice within the United States.

People, the P.A.G.C.H. is about eradiation hunger/starvation, but this would also require us to address other issues that can impede our purpose. This equally applies to domestic obstacles. We cannot keep blaming global racism. Especially when we are doing nothing to stop global racism directed at our Global Black Diaspora; propaganda/rhetoric doesn't fill emptied bellies. Our domestic stability will determine our global leadership and success. Please understand I realize this is a vast and intricate endeavor, and it may discourage many, but to end this crisis, it will take institutions, not programs, and this explains why the problem is persistent. Also, remember, because you may lack the vision to see this project as a reality, doesn't mean everybody else lack that same vision, so don't impose your blindness on those with the vision to breathe life into this global infrastructure.

Abdul Olugbala Shakur
Project Creator and Chief Consultant

General Council
Secretary General
Deputy General
Secretary of Interior
Secretary of Treasurer
Security Consultant
Chief Consultant
International Advisor
Secretary
Additional Members

Domestic Affairs Council
Chairperson
Vice Chairperson
Treasurer
Secretary
Strategist
Security Advisor
Consultant
Additional Members

Committee on International Affairs
Chairperson
Vice Chairperson

Treasurer
Security Consultant
Chief Strategist
Chief Counsel
Consultant
Additional Members

Advisory Council
Chief Consultant
Deputy Consultant
Additional Consultants/Advisors

Domestic Institutions and Programs
New Afrikan Farmers Adoption Program (NAFAP)
New Afrikan People's Farm (NAPF)
New Afrikan Community Hatcheries (NACH)
New Afrikan Community People's Market (NACPM)
New Afrikan Community Cafeterias (NACC)
New Afrikan Community Council on Urban Farming (NACCUF)
New Afrikan Community Council on Green Technology (NACCGT)
New Afrikan Community Water Conservation Department
(NACWCD)
New Afrikan Farmers Trade Committee (NAFTC)
New Afrikan Agriculture Trust Fund (NAATF)
Bunchy Carter Institute for Community Reconstruction (BCICR)

International Institutions
Pan-Afrikan World Bank for Development (PAWBD)
Pan-Afrikan Council on Infrastructural Development (PACID)
Pan-Afrikan Import and Export Commission (PAIEC)
Pan-Afrikan Commission on Natural Mineral Rights (PACNMR)
Pan-Afrikan Agriculture Development Commission (PAADC)
Global Black Diaspora Reparation Trust Fund (GBDRTF)

North Amerikkka Pan-Afrikan Congressional Caucus
This Caucus (NAPACC) will consist of representatives from several pro-
Pan-Afrikan Organizations across North Amerikkka. For example: New
Afrikan People's Organization, Pan Afrikan Association of Amerikkka,
National Black United Front, December 12th Movement and New

Afrikan Revolutionary Nationalist People's Party to name a few. **NO NON governmental organizations or entities will be associated with the NAPACC, nor any entity that promotes racism, capitalism, colonialism, neo-colonialism, or imperialism.**

This caucus will develop and establish our foreign policies and agenda. We will not allow the United States government to define our foreign enemies or friends. We will serve the interest of **ALL BLACK PEOPLE FROM MEXICO TO EUROPE, FROM AFRIKA TO NORTH AMERIKKKA.** We have the resources to mobilize our Global Black Diaspora. This caucus will not fall prey to the internal ills which plagues the Pan-Afrikan Congress and other Pan-Afrikan entities.

P.A.G.C.H. BASIC STRUCTURE AND RESPONSIBILITIES

General Council

The General Council will be the leading body responsible for building, organizing and leading the P.A.G.C.H. The General Council will consist of:

1. Secretary General
2. Deputy General
3. Secretary of Interior
4. Secretary of Treasurer
5. Chief Security Consultant
6. Chief Consultant
7. International Advisor
8. Secretary

The P.A.G.C.H. Headquarters will be located in the United States, which will include The Office of the General Council. Proposed Schedule: The General Council will meet Monday through Thursday, 8:00 am to 12:00 noon. These four (4) day sessions will take place at least twice a month or when circumstances dictate. We estimate it may take at least 10 to 20 years to firmly establish the P.A.G.C.H., and all its internal components. To facilitate this building process, during the 10 to

20-year period the eight essential positions listed above will be occupied only by New Afrikans/Afrikans who live in the U.S. After this building process three (3) of the positions will be available to all member countries. The following positions will be available only to those New Afrikans/Afrikans who live in the United States:

1. Secretary General
2. Deputy General
3. Secretary of Interior
4. Secretary of Treasurer

The Chief Consultant will remain a position only available to a New Afrikan Activist, for he/she is the facilitator of this endeavor. But every member country that is an official member of our P.A.G.C.H. will have a representative on the General Council.

Secretary General

Besides serving as the Chair of the General Council (GC), the Secretary General is also delegated with the responsibility of:

1. Coordinating all the councils, commissions, and departments under his/her direction
2. To seek and recruit other Afrikan-based countries to become members of our General Council, and
3. To establish and maintain a clear line of communication with member countries.

The Secretary General is also the official spokesperson of the P.A.G.C.H. when possible and needed. He/she will travel throughout the Global Black Diaspora speaking on the importance, purpose, and objectives of the P.A.G.C.H. After the 20 year building period, the Secretary General will become an elected position only open to New Afrikans/Afrikans living within the United States. The Secretary General will have term limit of five (5) years, no more than two terms.

Deputy General

Besides serving as the Vice Chair of the General Council he/she will chair the committee on International Affairs. The Deputy General will also be an elected position, with a five (5) year term limit, no more than two terms.

Secretary of Interior

Besides serving as the third highest ranking member on the General Council, he/she will Chair the Domestic Affairs Council. The Secretary of Interior will be an elected position, elected by the Domestic Affairs Council. This position will be available only to the New Afrikans/Afrikans who live in the United States. He/she will serve a six (6) year term limit, no more than three terms. The Deputy Secretary of Interior will serve as the Vice Chair of the Committee on International Affairs.

Secretary of Treasurer

The Secretary of Treasurer is also an elected position. A position elected by the Domestic Affairs Council. The Secretary of Treasurer will also serve as the treasurer of the Committee on International Affairs. The Secretary of Treasurer will be responsible for the daily budgeting of the P.A.G.C.H. raising funds for the P.A.G.C.H. but one of his/her primary responsibilities will, be serving as Executive Director of the Pan-Afrikan World Bank for Development. He/she will serve a four (4) year term, no more than three terms.

Chief Security Consultant

Throughout the Global Black Diaspora, there are several politically unstable member countries, but we must not allow that instability to impede our ability to reach those in immediate need of assistance. The security consultant will develop a comprehensive plan designed to address our security concerns in those areas where political or civil unrest or legitimate Revolutionary protest are taking place. The security consultant will identify all potential hot spots and develop a clear decision on the ground, providing a report every 60 days (or when necessary) to the Secretary General and the Chief Consultant and emergency updates when circumstances dictate. **Note: The U.S. government will not define our enemies.** The Chief Security Consultant will serve three (3) year terms, no more than three terms.

Chief Consultant

The Chief Consultant is the guardian of this proposal and proposed institutions it intends to build. His/her responsibility will consist of the following, but not limited to:

1. To ensure that all established rules, policies and protocols are adhered to.
2. To ensure that NO department or entity within the .A.G.C.H. deviate from our established intent and purpose.
3. To ensure that the P.A.G.C.H. will **NEVER** become a medium for promoting capitalism.
4. To ensure that the P.A.G.C.H. **NEVER** falls under the dictate of any religious doctrine (e.g., Islam, Judaism, Christianity).
5. To ensure that the P.A.G.C.H. remain under the direct supervision and control of New Afrikans within the U.S.

The Chief Consultant will also chair the Advisory Council (AC) he/she will also have a seat on the General Council and a representative from the Advisory Council will have a seat in every committee, commission, council, and/or department, **BOTH DOMESTICALLY AND INTERNATIONALLY. NOTE: Any committee, commission, council or department within the P.A.G.C.H.** that fails to consult the designated consultant or Advisor will be disciplined. Multiple violations as it pertains to this failure will result in the expulsion of those in charge. The Chief Consultant and the Advisory Council is the backbone to the success of this proposed institution. The Chief Consultant is appointed by the Secretary of Interior. He/she will serve a ten (10) year term, no more than two terms. The long term limit guarantees the continuity and stability as the P.A.G.C.H. experience the inevitability of transitions.

International Advisor

As its maturity this institution will be a global force and it will be imperative to our success we have both a functional and practical comprehension of the science and dynamics of geo political/economic issues. The International Advisor is to advise the General Council on the socio-political/economic dynamics of every member country and/or potential member country. The International Advisor will serve seven

(7) year term, no more than three terms. The General Council will appoint this position.

Secretary

Besides serving on the General Council and the responsibility that may entail, the Secretary will also serve as the Secretary for the North Amerikkka Pan-Afrikan Congressional Caucus (NAPAGC). The Secretary of Interior will appoint this term. The Secretary will have a three-year term, no more than three terms.

DOMESTIC AFFAIRS COUNCIL

The Domestic Affairs Council (DAC) implements the domestic agenda of the P.A.G.C.H. as previously stated. The council will be chaired by the Secretary of Interior. The DAC will implement the following agenda:

New Afrikan Farmers Adoption Program (NAFAP)

According to recent statistics, New Afrikan (Black) farmers account for less than 1% of farmers in Amerikkka. This is a tragic reality. Especially when in early 1900s, New Afrikans owned farmland had comprised of millions of acres. But, from 1920 to 1982, 94% of those farms were unjustly hijacked. Our lack of support for our New Afrikan farmers has only facilitated this rapid deterioration. The Domestic Affairs Council (DAC) will develop an adoption program. This is how we envision this adoption program. Let's say there are four (4) New Afrikan owned farms in the State of Georgia that agree to be part of the adoption program, each farm will be adopted by a city in that State that has a significant New Afrikan population. The City of Atlanta will adopt one; Decatur will adopt one; College Park will adopt one, and Gainesville will adopt the fourth farm. All the New Afrikans in those cities will support their adopted farms financially and in volunteer labor. In turn, the farmer will donate a portion of his/her farm to the Domestic Affairs Council, which will be used to grow food and raise livestock such as turkey, chicken, fish, and rabbit, without steroids or vegetables sprayed with poisonous insecticides.

New Afrikan People's Farm (NAPF)

One of the primary goals of the DAC is to develop the effective means of food production to distribute food items to our communities. At present, we depend totally on the government and other outside forces to feed our children/people. Food is a life sustaining necessity and we have placed our lives and that of our children in the hands of a capitalist system that doesn't care if our children live or die. The DAC intends to assume the responsibility of feeding our impoverished communities, and acquiring land is a prerequisite.

The DAC will purchase land in their jurisdiction (i.e. state). These lands will be designated the New Afrikan People's Farm (NAPF). These farms will also address other socio economic/political issues. For example: At least two (2) of the NAPF in each state will be designated the Sojourner Truth Farm School. The Farm Schools primary focus will be our young people from the age of 10 to 17. At least one of these Farm Schools will focus on our homeless New Afrikan Youth. We will have two dormitories built on this farm, one for female and one for males between the ages of 12 and 17 years old. The dormitories will provide these young homeless brothers and sisters with decent shelter and three nutritional meals. They will also have to work and farm the land. They will be responsible for the daily maintenances of the food crops and livestock. Through their direct participation, we hope to return them back to the natural order of things. For one, a responsibility and a sense of purpose. The Sojourner Truth Farm School (STFS) will also provide classes in Afro-Centric/Pan-Afrikan Studies, computer training, science, math, writing, English, physical fitness/self-defense, and other significant vocational training. We also intend to designate at least one People's Farm in each state, the Bunchy Carter Collective Training Facility (BCCTF). These facilities will be specifically for training and preparing New Afrikan Prisoners just released. These brothers and sisters must farm the land and participate in the educational, vocational, and training courses that will be available at the BCCTF.

New Afrikan Community Hatcheries (NACH)

Some of the People's Farms will be partitioned for the development of hatcheries. We will produce our own eggs, (e.g., chickens, turkey, duck). These will be small and organic operated hatcheries, having little to no impact on our environment. We will also raise our own fish to provide for our people/community and for sale. The Domestic Affairs Council (DAC) will also purchase fishing boats to compliment this endeavor. We hope to make fish an important part of our People's daily diet. New Afrikan Community People's Markets (NACPM). The DAC hope to open People's Markets throughout the New Afrikan community. These people's Markets will provide fresh, safe, and affordable food items. The majority of the grocery stores in our communities are owned by non-New Afrikans. People who live outside of our community who don't give a damn about our daily struggle, plus the outrageous prices and lack of respect for our community/People. The DAC will establish our own community-based markets filled with the food items we raised and grow on the New Afrikan People's Farm and import from those member countries within our Global Black Diaspora. Certain families, based on their annual income, will receive a bag of free food items every week until their financial situation improves. But we will take care of our elders.

New Afrikan Community Cafeterias (NACC)

Instead of depending on soup kitchens or government-sponsored handouts, we will develop community-based cafeterias. The NACC will not replace cooking at home, nor will they accommodate lazy parents. These cafeterias will only serve those families and individuals in need of such services. The NACC will serve those families and individuals that meet our standard criteria. This is a brief example:

    a. Their annual income is under the national poverty line, as defined by our Domestic Affairs Council.

    b. Those temporarily unemployed.

    c. Those who suffer from medical/health problems, serious injuries or mental disorders. We will also make home deliveries to the sick, handicapped, and elderly.

d. Children/Youth whose parents work at certain hours that prevents them from cooking meals at the appropriate time.

As I stated, the NACC will not be exploited by lazy or irresponsible parents. Every individual/family the NACC serves will be assigned according to the information provided in their required application form. Once their application form is processed and evaluated by the NACC staff, the individual/family will be given a cafeteria schedule based on the information provided via their application form. For example: a single father with two children can only provide two decent meals such as breakfast and lunch. NACC will provide the third meal (dinner). This father will be issued a cafeteria pass only for dinner. Though only People with a cafeteria pass may eat at the NACC, we will deny no family or individual in need.

*These procedures are only designed to minimize abuse of the NACC. The NACC is not a medium to reward laziness, poor work ethic or parental irresponsibility.

New Afrikan Community Council on Urban Farming

The value of functional knowledge becomes self-evident when we see New Afrikan families suffering from lack of food, but yet have significant yard space occupied by weeds and non-reciprocated vegetation. Not realizing a partial solution to their immediate need is right in front of them. The NACCUF's primary objective will be two-fold:

1. To educate and train our community to the science of urban gardening, using both green technology and organic methods as their guiding principles.

2. To train the community on how to utilize every designated space to grow both vegetables and fruit trees, transforming the entire community, especially those in need. This objective equally applies to areas that are primarily concrete. To accommodate these conditions, we must employ our ingenuity towards developing an effective method to maximizing the limited space that would allow us to produce food in these types of environment; green housing and hydroponic gardening are

just some of the methods that will compensate for the lack of top soil.

New Afrikan Community Council on Green Technology (NACGT)

It is imperative towards our sustained longevity for us as a community to develop and implement Green-Technology in the service of our PAGCH. Our interest not only lies in protecting our environment but equally important to our sustainability is cost. Green Technology will give a dramatic impact on our capacity to effectively fund all institutions and programs related to our domestic division. Developing more effective and sufficient methods in collecting rain water will be a priority for the NACGT. As well as employing solar and wind energy to serve both our People's Farms and community-based businesses and homes. We will not just depend on others for this technology, we will also get in the business of developing Green-Technology, especially for farming.

New Afrikan Community Water Conservation Department (NACWCD)

We live in a society where the government, along with big corporations, has lost all concern for the People, especially poor People of color. Almost every other month we hear how some big corporation or government-sponsored project has dumped hazardous waste in the drinking water, jeopardizing the health and safety of an entire community/city. Water is a life giving necessity bestowed upon all humankind, not a select few. We have every right to protect the water supply. No one (including government) can claim absolute proprietorship over water. The Domestic Affairs Council (DAC) via this Department will establish community-based facilities designed to conserve and guarantee the New Afrikan Community an emergency safe water supply.

New Afrikan Farmers Trade Committee (NAFTC)

Due to the inherent institutionalized racism which plagues the U.S., New Afrikan (Black) farmers have been systematically overlooked, if not dismissed altogether, as it pertains to selling their food items to the open-market, may it be in the domestic market or international markets. The Trade Committee will represent all the New Afrikan People's farms. The NAFTC will establish business transactions between the New Afrikan People's Farms (NAPF) and supermarkets, restaurants, grocery stores, the school districts, colleges and universities. The New Afrikan Farmers Trade Committee will also work closely with our Committee on International Affairs in developing a program that would permit New Afrikan Farmers to sell their food products to other countries including on the continent of Europe, South Amerikkka, Asia, and the entire Black Global Diaspora, including Afrika.

New Afrikan Agriculture Trust Fund (NAATF)

One of the main factors which have facilitated the rapid demise of New Afrikan Farmers in the U.S. is the lack of funds. The banks refusal to give New Afrikan farmer's loans, plus government contracts, and regulations are designed to force the New Afrikan farmers to foreclose or turnover their farm due to debts. This is a brief example of how this government has sponsored racist-based fascist agendas designed to reduce New Afrikan owned farmland. The Domestic Affairs Council (DAC) will develop a New Afrikan Agriculture Trust Fund. This trust fund will not only support our New Afrikan People's Farms; it will also purchase/acquire land to expand on our Agrarian Revolution. The NAATF will under no circumstances accept funds or grants from, the government or government special interest groups. We will utilize several methods for raising funds. For example: Asking our People throughout the country to make a monthly charitable donation from .50 to $1.00, whatever each family/individual can afford to give.

Bunchy Carter Institute for Community Reconstruction (BCICR)

We can no longer afford to depend on others to think for us, we understand our situation better than anyone. The solution(s) to our day-to-day problems lies within our functional understanding of the internal dynamics which govern the rules of cause and effect. What is apparent, are the effects, such as poverty, hunger, high blood pressure, obesity, violence, etc., etc., etc., but what is the cause (s) to the manifestation of these material/physical expressed symptoms? Only we as a community are qualified to diagnose both the cause and affects. The BCICR will serve as community-based think tanks, the community will select eleven (11) known community activists from their community to serve as their think tank under the BCICR. They will analyze every problem facing that particular community and provide concrete analyses and solutions to these problems, each community also has its own unique problems, but all community-based BCICR will work together, and share analysis and ideas, as well as provide their community with an update assessment of the conditions of the community.

The community-based BCICR will have an elected chairperson, vice-chair, and they will appoint their own Treasurer, Secretary, and Community Facilitator. The BCICR will not work with the government or law enforcement, nor will it accept government funding. Our goal is to emancipate our community from depending on the government and law enforcement. It's time to be the masters of our own destiny.

COMMITTEE ON INTERNATIONAL AFFAIRS

The Committee on International Affairs (COIA) implements the International agenda of the PAGCH. Its responsibility is multi-dimensional, but eradicating hunger and starvation within our Global Black Diaspora is the primary focus of the committee. But its other objectives are equally important. The following institutions will be accountable to this committee. The Deputy Secretary General will chair this committee, and the Deputy Secretary of Interior will serve as the Vice-Chair.

Pan-Afrikan World Bank for Development (PAWBD)

Despite the United Nation International Monetary Fund (UNIMF) and the International Bank for Reconstruction and Development (IBRD), also known as The World Bank, the majority of the countries within our Global Black Diaspora face a pandemic of poverty and starvation. The rapid deterioration of vital infrastructure and extreme foreign debts has forced many countries within our Global Black Diaspora (GBD) to capitulate to the dictates of European-Imperialism (Amerikkka in particular) which is not in their/or our best interest. These institutions (i.e. UNIMF and IBRD) have not served in our best interest as a global Black Diaspora. They have only made us more dependent on European/foreign assistance while our internal crisis goes unsolved.

It is time for our Global Black Diaspora to develop our own International World Bank. This will be one of the primary objectives of the COIA. The Pan-Afrikan World Bank for development will be our bank. It will provide member countries with loans at reasonable interest rates. It will also invest in businesses owned by members of our GBD which encompasses gold and diamond mines, oil fields and high-tech. There will be a twenty (20) year freeze on the Pan-Afrikan World Bank for Development (PAWBD). **No money** will be withdrawn from the PAWBD during this 20-year period (unless in case of emergency: The General Council Secretary of Treasurer will determine the particulars). We will use this period to establish our Global World Bank. Many have asked where the funds will come from. We will employ several methods.

For example:
1. We will collect reparations from all countries that had participated and profited from the Afrikan-Slave trade;
2. To demand compensation from those countries via fraud and/or Kolonialism that have control over Afrikan mineral rights which includes oil and natural gas;
3. Every member country in our General Council must pay a membership fee every six (6) months. The amount will be determined by the General Council;
4. Donations
5. Profits from our investments.

This was/is a preliminary list. **THE PAWBD WILL NOT BE A KAPITALISTIC INSTITUTION**, it will function on an Afrikan-rooted concept of equalitarianism e.g. Cooperative
economics and collective work and responsibility (Ujamaa & Ujima). The PAWBD will be under the direction of the Secretary of Treasurer.

Pan-Afrikan Council on Infrastructural Development (PACID)

The most common characteristics shared by many countries where hunger/starvation are constant pandemics, is their infrastructures are rapidly deteriorating, or basically non-existent, and without the adequate infrastructure it becomes a protracted and complicated endeavor to feed all their at-risk population. This also affects their capacity to accommodate outside help and our collaborative effort to feed, defend, or employ their citizens. The PACID will focus on developing and establishing these infrastructures in our member countries:

A. All infrastructures related to the cultivation, production, distribution and preservation of food.
B. Decent shelter, housing and apartment complexes.
C. Education system: Preschool to College.
D. Technology: Green-technology.
E. Health/Medical Care
F. Economic Development

Afrika has a vast desert that can be transformed into massive solar and wind farms. Note: We intend to operate independent from political corruption and dictators. We equally realize it won't be easy.

Pan-Afrikan Import and Export Commission (PAIEC)

The global marketing is primarily controlled and under the dictate of a capitalist oligarchy, e.g. the United States, China, Britain, Germany, France, Italy and Japan. And the Global Black Diaspora (GBD) is not only the most exploited but *the* most neglected; it is a primary contributing factor in its weakened economy and global economic and political influence.

Effectively importing and exporting goods between countries within our GBD would contribute towards the growth and stability of each local economy, while simultaneously strengthening our position within the global market. The PAIEC will be designed to help each member country improve their import and export capability, along with the quality of their exported goods from food products to technology. It is important to note, the PAIEC will not serve as a medium to promote a kapatalistic approach towards global market development.

Pan-Afrikan Commission on Natural Mineral Rights (PACNMR)

Under the oppressive system of Kolonialism, (i.e., Colonialism), and Neo-Kolonialism, foreign governments and their business communities could outright steal land and hijack mineral rights from Afrika to the Caribbean. The PACNMR will develop a global coalition of Attorneys and activists committed to restoring rightful ownership of land, mineral rights, and oil fields back to our People. This also includes land the U.S. stolen from our Global Black Diaspora.

Pan-Afrikan Agriculture Development Commission (PAADC)

As I stated at the onset, starvation/and hunger are preventable social diseases, not only in the U.S. and other European countries/or countries under their controlled have only played politics with this human crisis. For the most part, the United Nations (U.N.) and other international so-called humanitarian organizations, only ship food to these stricken areas which do not solve the problem. Our GBD needs to develop our own source of food. The PAADC will initiate and establish an agricultural educational program throughout the GBD.

This program will consist of:
1. Sending a team of experienced New Afrikan/Black farmers (or any farmers willing to volunteer their expertise), to the member countries to teach the People how to efficiently, organically (and environmental safely) cultivate the land and the science of agriculture.
2. Ship farm equipment and seeds to these member countries.
3. Develop irrigation systems (i.e., based on green-technology) to water their vegetables and fruit trees, and livestock, but more important, to provide clean and safe drinking water for their families and rural villages and towns.

4. To establish a local program designed to feed their People and make them less dependent on foreign hand-outs with hidden agendas.

Global Black Diaspora Reparation Trust Fund (GBDRTF)

Many European countries such as Portugal, Spain, France, Britain, Italy, and the United States (to name a few) strong economies are rooted in the genocidal-system of slavery. These countries enjoyed hundreds of years of the accumulation of stolen material wealth and forced free labor, and got away with the **Murder, Rape, Child Molestation and Torture of an entire race of Pe**ople, but yet feel no obligation of recompense? Afrika became impoverished and the pandemic of wealth depletion is directly linked to the genocidal system of Slavery and Kolonial conquest. The GBDRTF **will seek and demand reparations from all countries, industries, companies, and/or People** who have (and continue) to benefit from the system of genocidal-system of Slavery and Kolonial oppression. It is time for all involved to take responsibility for their crimes against Mother-Afrika/Humanity. And for the U.S., let me emphasize this point, you participated in this genocide as a country and not as individual citizens. Your Congress and Supreme Court made decisions supporting Slavery and **Jim Crow**. They gave it legal legitimacy, an atrocity approved by your government and stolen country. We demand reparation from the U.S. government as an institution and those companies/industries who had, and continue to benefit from, the Black Afrikan Holocaust, which includes over one hundred years of Jim Crow. Must we remind you according to your own laws; there is **NO** statute of limitations for MURDER, AND MILLIONS HAD DIED AS A DIRECT RESULT OF THE ATLANTIC SLAVE-TRADE. The Funds from the GBDRTF will assist in building our Global Black Diaspora.

CONCLUSION

I understand this is a vast project that will warrant mass mobilization. People, this is only a blue-print; it is to be implemented in stages. The first stage is the Urban Garden programs. We must identify every available space in our communities exposed to direct sun-light and plant vegetables and fruit trees, e.g. Pinto Beans, White Bean, Black Eyed Peas, String Beans, Sweet Peas, Corn, Tomatoes, Collard Greens, Mustard Greens, Carrots, Apple Trees, Orange Trees, Grapefruit Trees, to name a few. Go to each neighbor and discuss transforming the entire community into a source for feeding our children. Some families can raise chickens for eggs and meat, some can even go fishing on behalf of the community. Our think-tank is presently developing methods that will allow our People living in housing projects and apartment/housing complexes to cultivate their own food crops; roof-top gardening is just one of multiple methods we are assessing. This first stage is imperative to the success of this proposed plan. It helps to develop a collective consciousness that breathe life into the fundamental concept of developing our own institutions committed to feeding our children, People, community and Global Black Diaspora.

A few years back I was watching a "feed the children" infomercial and Pastor Scott's wife was talking to a Black Single Mother of two. They were sitting on the front porch, but what caught my attention was I noticed the Sista had significant back yard space and side yard space. The Sista did not realize a partial solution to her problem lies in her own hands, but she had lacked the consciousness that would have allowed her to utilize her yard space to grow vegetables and raise chickens. This first stage is essential towards developing the conscious concept of living off the land.

My People, my name is ABDUL OLUGBALA SHAKUR. I am a New Afrikan Freedom Fighter, and a Political Prisoner of war in the service of the New Afrikan Independence Movement (NAIM). I have spent the last 32 years in solitary confinement/isolation. I am the Chief Coordinator and Executive Director of an imprisoned Think-tank, the Concrete Scholars Foundation (CSF). We develop analyses and proposed solutions about the problems facing Afrikan/Black People around the world; in particular, the U.S. This proposal is just one of many we have developed in the service of our People.

The success of this proposed plan depends on what we do as a People. We cannot blame others for our failure to act in our own best interest; I challenge you to do these things:

1. If you are a New Afrikan activist (s), I encourage you to take this proposal to the community and initiate community-based study groups designed to implement this proposal.
2. If you are a New Afrikan college student, convince/or encourage your Black Student Union (BSU) to embrace and sponsor this proposal
3. Distribute copies of this proposal in your area
4. If you wish to be an official coordinator for this project, contact me directly.

NOTE:

The U.S. government or advocates of the U.S. Kapitalist system of human exploitation will not play a role in this institution. Due to certain laws and treaties, we understand we will be forced to eventually work with the government on certain matters, but we will not allow any government or industry/businesses to exploit the poor People connected to this institution, or any poor People. This institution is not about profiting off of poor people, poverty, or poor countries. We also intend to file with the United Nations (U.N.) as a NGO (Non-Governmental-Organization.

Marcus Garvey Study Group

Participant Guide Booklet

We as a People are still suffering from both the psychological and physical effects of racial oppression in Amerikkka.

—–Abdul Olugbala Shakur

Marcus Garvey Study Group

Preamble

The intellectual capacity to compete with any race and transform our community into 21st century pyramids starts with knowing who we are as a People. If we know the truth about our history, we can learn we need not resort to criminal behavior to survive in a society still filled with racism. Without knowledge of our true selves, we are vulnerable to the trappings and seductions of the criminal/gangster mentality.

In an effort to transform this way of thinking and eradicate the slave mentality, we have developed the Marcus Garvey Study Group (MGSG), which intertwines components of the Black Progressive Prison Rights Movement and the George Jackson University (GJU). Our project will coexist between the Prison Industrial Slave Complex (PISC), and our Communities.

In analyzing the Willie Lynch system/method for breaking an Afrikan slave, it becomes clear how imperative it was for the genocidal architects of the system of slavery to strip our Ancestors of their true cultural identity. Little did our ancestors realize that their susceptibility to the slave mentality would permeate into the future for generations to come. This slave-mentality can be seen in the way it has catapulted into contemporary times, despite resistance from many of our Ancestors; from the poor conditions of our people, to the negro President Barak Obama, and the young Brother in the hood who believes he must sell drugs to his People to survive, or kill other Brothers because they come from a different neighborhood.

We have been orientated to hate ourselves, and our own Blackness, so we attempt to impersonate others, like Italian gangsters, and call ourselves Capone, Scarface, Lefty, and Gotty, to name a few – never considering the names embodying our greatness such as Queen Nzinga, Shaka Zulu, Assata Shakur, and Nehanda Abiodun.

While mainstream society refuses to accept the role and/or impact the Genocidal system of Slavery, or Jim Crow, has had on the Collective psyche of our Ancestors, and how their role has transcended each generation, we cannot allow ourselves to be bullied out of this, our truth and reality.

This project has several objectives besides its design to challenge and optimistically eradicate the Black Criminal/Gangster mentality. The MGSG intends to address all these issues by bringing our history back to the forefront of our minds and lives and transforming the slave mentality to not only write our new history, but combine it with the truth about our past.

Program Overview

Upon approval of an MGSG Cadre, they will be placed on a rooster with a registration number:

1. Each MGSG Cadre cannot exceed ten individuals.
2. Each individual must write a ten (10) page essay on the book they were assigned to read.
3. Upon receipt of a completed essay, the MGSG Cadre will receive their next book. If an essay is not turned in due to refusal of completing one, the Cadre will be removed from the group.

We cannot accomplish this task alone, so we are humbly petitioning for the support of individuals and/or groups who will volunteer their time to serve as either sponsors or donors or both.

Donor Responsibilities

The Donor will be responsible for purchasing books from our approved Book List that is designated to various MGSG's. Donor purchases of the required books from Black owned bookstores will benefit their businesses, creating mediums for others to visit their stores and continue to build upon these purchases.

***Marcus Garvey Study Group Top Ten Required Books (see next two attachments for book list and bookstores):**

Note: The Donor will purchase book(s) directly from Black owned bookstores only in order to support Black owned businesses. The book store will mail the book to each individual registered in that particular MGSG. We will provide the donor with the names and addresses of each individual in a particular MGSG Cadre.

Sponsorship Responsibilities

- A Sponsor is an individual and/or group who agree to sponsor the MGSG project. This sponsorship will consist of:
    - Providing the necessary resources to sustain the project.
    - To become fundraisers on behalf of the MGSG project.
    - To assist us in providing supplies to indigent participants, such as
        - Writing Tablets.
        - Manila Envelopes.
        - Business Size Envelopes.
        - Stamps/Stamped Envelopes.
        - Donate Computers, Printers, Copiers and Filing Cabinets, and other office supplies to the outside MGSG Coordinating Committee (MGSG-CC).

We are also looking for outside Coordinators, volunteers and support. This project cannot be maintained without a committed support network, if you are interested in volunteering you can get at us via one of the below addresses.

Basic Protocols

Under no circumstances are participants allowed to engage in:

- Criminal/gang activities.
- The using or selling of PCP, Meth/Acid, Cocaine, Heroin or misuse of prescription drugs.
- The abuse, harm, sexual assault or disrespect of children, women, or elders.

Sponsored by: Black Progressive Prison Rights Movement (BPPRM)
George Jackson University (GJU).

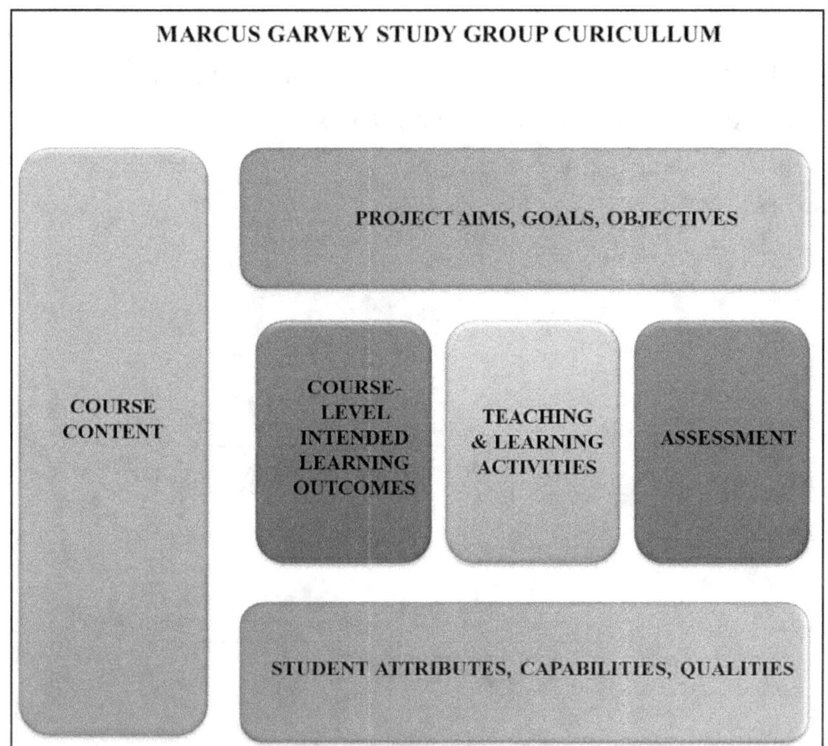
MARCUS GARVEY STUDY GROUP CURICULLUM
PROJECT AIMS, GOALS, OBJECTIVES
COURSE CONTENT
COURSE-LEVEL INTENDED LEARNING OUTCOMES
TEACHING & LEARNING ACTIVITIES
ASSESSMENT
STUDENT ATTRIBUTES, CAPABILITIES, QUALITIES

WHAT IS A THESIS STATEMENT?

- Typically it is one sentence but sometimes more may be needed.
- It states the main idea or argument of your essay.
- It lets your reader know what to expect.
- It is the basis for your entire essay.
- It is the most important part of your essay.
- It is impressive.

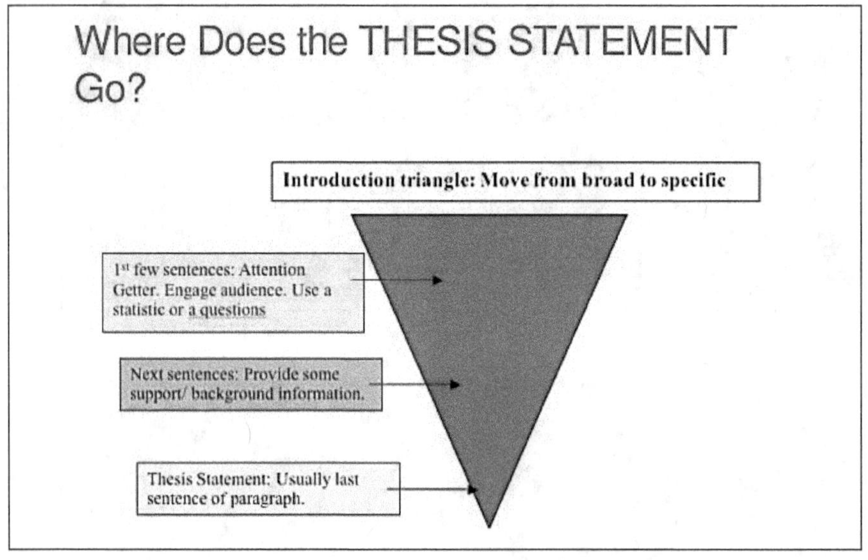

Topic

Attention Getter:

Thesis:

Point 1

Point 2

Point 3

Support/examples

Support/examples

Support/examples

Conclusion

Marcus Garvey Study Group Required Book List

1. *Two Thousand Seasons* by Ayi Kwei Armah focuses on the complicity of African people to the enslavement of their people to intruders. In doing so, the novel emphasizes the continued complicity of African leaders in furthering the oppression of other African peoples.

2. *The Destruction of Black Civilization* was written at a time when many black students, educators, and scholars were starting to piece together the connection between the way their history was taught and the way they were perceived by others and by themselves. They began to question assumptions made about their history and took it upon themselves to create a new body of historical research. The book is premised on the question: "If the Blacks were among the very first builders of civilization and their land the birthplace of civilization, what has happened to them that has left them since then, at the bottom of world society?"

3. *The African Origin of Civilization* by Cheikh Anta Diop: Now in its 30th printing, this classic presents historical, archaeological, and anthropological evidence to support the theory that ancient Egypt was a black civilization.

4. *David Walker's Appeal* is a landmark work of American history and letters, the most radical piece of writing by an African American in the nineteenth century. Startling in its intensity, unrelenting in its attacks on slavery and white racism, it alarmed Southern slaveholders, inspired Northern abolitionists, and hastened the sectional conflicts that led to the Civil War.

5. In *Gabriel's Rebellion,* Douglas R. Egerton analyzes two important slave revolts of the early 19th century as having to do with economics and class as much as with slavery and race. The more important of the two revolts was led by Gabriel Prosser, a much mythologized figure whom Egerton tries to recover from his murky past.

6. *The Condition, Elevation, Emigration, and Destiny of the Colored People of the United States* by Martin R. Delany: African American abolitionist, author, public intellectual, physician, the highest ranking black officer during the Civil War, and a notable activist for the emigration of blacks to Africa, Martin Robison Delany has left an enduring legacy in his writings, the power of his ideas, and his political activism. So influential was he during the nineteenth century that a number of people now refer to him as the "Father of Black Nationalism."

7. *Denmark Vesey: The Buried Story of America's Largest Slave Rebellion and the Man Who Led It.* In a remarkable feat of historical detective work, David Robertson illuminates the shadowy figure who planned a slave rebellion so daring that, if successful, it might have changed the face of the antebellum South.

8. *Nat Turner and the Southampton campaign of the Black Liberation Army in 1831*; a slave rebellion that took place in Southampton County, Virginia, in August 1831 led by Nat Turner. Rebel slaves killed from 55 to 65 people, at least 51 being white. The rebellion was put down within a few days, but Turner survived in hiding for more than two months afterwards.

9. *Negroes with Guns* is a 1962 book by civil rights activist Robert F. Williams. It is an intellectual influence on Huey P. Newton, the founder of the "Black Panther Party." The book is used in college courses, and is discussed in current debates. When many black students, educators, and scholars were starting to piece together the connection between the way their history was taught and the way they were perceived by others and by Assata: This intensely personal and political autobiography belies the fearsome image of JoAnne Chesimard long projected by the media and the state. With wit and candor, Assata Shakur recounts the experiences that led her to a life of activism and portrays the strengths, weaknesses, and eventual demise of Black and White revolutionary groups at the hand of government officials.

Black Owned Bookstore Website Links

https://pyramidbooks.indielite.org/
http://www.blackclassicbooks.com/
https://www.esowonbookstore.com/
http://www.sourcebooksellers.com/
http://nandisknowledgecafe.com/
http://blackartplus.com/
https://www.facebook.com/marcus.books/
https://www.mahoganybooks.com/
https://www.thedockbookshop.com/
https://www.facebook.com/Zawadi-Books 466887943377904/
https://www.blackandnobel.com/collections/ knowledge-books-1
https://www.facebook.com/LaUniqueAfrican/
https://blackworldbooks.org/
https://www.cafeconlibrosbk.com/
https://harambeebooks.org/
https://darebooks.com/
https://www.unclebobbies.com/
https://hakimsbookstore.com/
https://www.events.sankofa.com/blank
https://www.facebook.com/Nubian Bookstore-110668169013960/

STRATEGIC EARLY RELEASE PROGRAM

Proposed Proposition - 2020

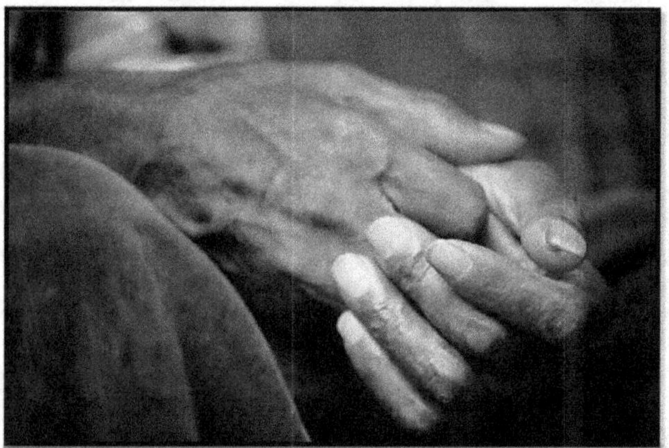

Abdul Olugbala Shakur

Joka Heshima Jinsai

Strategic Early Release Program
Proposed Proposition 2020

Preamble

The Prisoner cohort with the *lowest* recidivism rate, which we term the **Strategic Release Class,** is the indeterminate, or life term Prisoner over 50 who has served 25 years or more of continuous confinement. The recidivism rate in this group is only *.015%*; it is virtually non-existent. Despite this, the **Strategic Release Class** is *not* the focus of the Government/California Department of Corrections (CDCr) when initiating several rounds of early release programs designed to alleviate over-crowding in its facilities.

In stark contrast, and in each instance as though it's some political magic bullet, the cohort of focus for release are non-violent Prisoners; drug offenders, or determinate term offenders with 24 months or less remaining on their terms. Understand, the non-violent drug offender, and low-based term determinate sentence offender cohort has a 60% to 70% recidivism rate (Re-offending for this cohort appears to increase in the summer months based on the findings of the Bureau of Justice Statistics).

The most recent early release program reduces the chance of rapid transmission of Corona Virus (COVID-19) during the pandemic. We can only conclude, based on the numbers from the Bureau of Justice Statistics, this cohort of Prisoners is the main focus of Prison Industrialists because of one or both:

1. It sounds less threatening to legislators and the public.
2. By intentionally focusing on the cohort of prisoners when referencing these groups to legislators and the Governor, in which the majority will re-offend, the objective is to sabotage the entire premise of early release programs.

The **Strategic Release Class** described above have dedicated themselves to the social, economic, political/cultural development, and positive progress of their communities and society, making them not only the obvious public safety selection, but an actual asset to all of us upon release.

Due to decades of imprisonment, relative maturity and development, and the increased value they place on freedom and community ties (based on their advanced age), the **Strategic Release Class** simply does not re-offend. If we look further into this cohort and consider those long-term offenders with a proven record of service to their communities and society over the course of decades (as evidenced by their work productivity), their negligible recidivism rate drops to 0%.

If public safety is the primary concern of the CDCr, legislators, and the Governor in early release programs, and not just politically safe language, the primary cohort focus of early release programs should be the **Strategic Release Class**, the aged 50+ indeterminate term cohort.

In the current crises, this cohort of Prisoners are at great risk of severe complications or death during the COVID-19 pandemic due to over-crowed prison conditions. Of equal importance, this cohort has the greatest number of job skills, experience, and accumulated knowledge, bringing meaningful contributions to their communities and job markets. By any measure, it is this long-term offender cohort, the **Strategic Release Class,** who should be the primary focus of ongoing early release programs.

–Joka Heshima Jinsai

Proposed Proposition

It has been well established and documented by state and federal statistics, the present primary demographics targeted for the Governor/CDCr early release programs due to COVID-19 are the demographics which possess the highest recidivism rate. We are wondering: is this a deliberate scheme initiated by the Democratic and Republican Parties to undermine the very concept of early release for Prisoners by dismissing the fact that poor communitiesand society suffer the most because of this political error – or scam – in disguise?

Many of the recently released inmates who were housed in county jail facilities are re-offending with violent crime(s), and these cases are being used as examples of why these programs should not exist by those who oppose such programs and/or legislation. For example, in the area I currently reside, an inmate was arrested for an alleged rape and for beating his wife four (4) times within six weeks. This case is now being used by law enforcement as the benchmark for why such programs and/or legislations do not work.

Close to 40 years ago I came to prison, and along with our class of the Conscious Prisoners Council of Elders, we acknowledge when many of us were much younger and entered the Prison Industrial Slave Complex (PISC), we had no discipline, and lacked remorse for the things we actually did, but our unique class of Conscious Elder Prisoners have dedicated our service toward building our Communities, which encompasses transforming the Black Criminal/Gangster Mentality. Today, we would be an asset towards building a better community for our People to live in.

Drawing from our collective experiences, the Conscious Prisoners Council of Elders offer the following proposed proposition in response to the present failed concept of early release in order to eliminate potential threats to communities and society, by proposing the Government/CDCr focus on a much safer demographic for their early release programs:

PROPOSED PROPOSITION CRITERIA

1. Above the age of 50.
2. Served at least 27 years in prison.
3. Are presently involved in a proven stable relationship, such as marriage, but not necessarily limited to marriage; long-term being the key factor.
4. Have strong family ties or community-based support.
5. He/she must be employable in order to be self-sufficient.
6. Provide examples of years of giving back to the communities.
7. Must not have sexual assault related criminal record.

> Note: The above criterion does not apply to our proposition. There would not be a flood of Prisoners released as it would concern less than 1% of prisoners, however, the positive impact they would have on communities and society would be 100-fold. We also suggest releasing the top two to three proven candidates who meet the above criteria and observe their achievements in their first year.

With these criteria, the chance of re-offending becomes almost non-existent, and the community will receive a class of prisoners who have shown their ongoing commitment to building their respective communities and society. The Government can develop an independent panel consisting of three (3) people who will review those Prisoners seeking relief/release under these new standards, and the community should have input regarding who the prisoners might be released to. The panel decision must be based on the facts, such as the above criteria, and not on a narrative(s) provided by the CDCr.

We are presently distributing copies of this proposal throughout the Afrikan-Amerikan communities, encouraging them to become sponsors of this proposal, and if necessary, introduce it as a potential bill to be placed on the ballot for the People to vote on.

Abdul Olugbala Shakur

OPERATION HIP-HOP RESCUE
"A MOVEMENT"

"Black on Black Gang and Drug related violence can only be resolved by us, both as a People and Community, and not by working with the cops or the government"
— Abdul Olugbala Shakur

Presented by: Abdul Olugbala Shakur
aka J. Harvey

Sponsored by:
The Black Progressive Prison Rights Movement
BPPRM

Every problem has a history, a beginning, an infant stage, and a path of its growth and development; a maturity.
- Abdul Olugbala Shakur

Operation Hip-Hop Rescue
"A Movement"

Preamble

Our goal is to transform the Black Street Organization (i.e. Gang) and eliminate the negative aspects of the street organizations, our goal and programs are designed to achieve this desired effect. The key to an effective program(s), it must first attract the Gang members attention in a positive way, if not, your effort will prove fruitless. The cornerstone of Operation Hip-Hop Rescue (OHHR) is directly based on the positive inclinations of New Afrikan (aka Afrikan-Amerikkkan) street organizations, and it is their collective love and appreciation for Rap/and the hip-hop culture.

When many of our people reviewed the original draft of this proposal, their criticism was: we as a People did not have the financial/material resources to invest in such a vast Plan of Action (POA). For me, this criticism REPRESENTED A VERY SAD, IF NOT PATHETIC commentary on our inability to relinquish the slave-mentality, which is to serve and enrich others while simultaneously *killing ourselves.* For the most part, we can invest millions, if not billions of dollars in fake hair/weaves, fake nails, fake breasts, cosmetic surgery, jewelry, clothes, shoes, tennis shoes, cars, marijuana, alcohol, strip-clubs, pornography, but we don't have the funds to invest in saving our children, community and/or future generations?

If this is not the mentality of a slave, then I do not know what is. I refuse to surrender to the reasoning of a slave-mentality. I am re-introducing this revised edition hoping to mobilize our people, community, and resources. We can show you how this plan of action can be implemented in stages and how we can raise the funds/resources.

People, because you may not be able to see how it can be done, does not mean everybody else is blind to its potential and/or implementation/applications. I ask what is more important. Saving our children, community, and future generations, or partying and wasting money on nonsense? This plan of operation is just one of many proposed solutions our collective has developed. However, we understand this plan of action is not the sole solution to this crisis.

Mission Statement

Many People have asked what is unique about Black-on-Black violence, especially when statistics reflect the vast majority of the assailants of Mexican victims of violence/murders were also Mexicans. This equally applies to Whites, Latinos, and Asians. Black on-Black violence only becomes unique when analyzed within its proper context and perspective, and this encompasses its historical implications and significance; the entire spectrum of its totality. A concrete understanding derives from a concrete analysis of all those elements conducive toward contributing factors as it pertains to the manifestation of the Black-on-Black violence phenomenon.

Let's first be clear. When we speak about Black-on-Black violence in this Mission Statement, we are primarily speaking about gang violence; however, this does not negate or diminish the significance of other forms of violence between our people. There are several areas worthy of our devoted attention, but gang violence is killing and injuring our people, Black Children/Youth, at an alarming rate. Our present objective is dedicated toward eradicating this aspect of Black-on-Black violence.

The present method being employed to address the gang violence for the most part has failed. The reasons vary, but the primary reason for this failure is due to the method. This method(s) is not ours, nor is it based on the concrete analysis of the concrete conditions in our communities. The method(s) is coming from outside of our communities, (government and law enforcement in particular), and their methods encompass incarceration over education, imprisonment over employment, and brutality over humanity. We need to develop our own methods for resolving this crisis, and who understands this problem better than us?

The quintessential factor when developing a solution to a problem is having a functional comprehension of the problem, and this includes all internal and external elements somehow contributing to either the manifestation of the problem or its proliferation. This is where a clear knowledge of our history becomes a prerequisite.

The gang problem/violence is no exception to this rule. Often when we scientifically examine and explore in retrospection, we are usually accused of looking for excuses for this violent behavior, or playing the blame game, which is contrary to this deliberate distortion of our endeavors. We as New Afrikan Activists understand to resolve the Black-on-Black gang violence (i.e. epidemic) we must chart its evolutionary development – its history. It's from this thorough analysis that allows us to develop a concrete solution.

Before I lay out what we believe is the most effective method for resolving Black gang violence, allow me to briefly expound on some of the key analyses that helped to shape and influence our approach and methods for this problem:

1. We did not bring the gang mentality to this country; it was already part of the Neo-European (i.e. Whites in Amerikkka) socio-cultural norms.
2. It was during the 1920s and 1930s, when our people lived in poverty, they became attracted to the gangster life-style to improve their financial situation.
3. During the 1960s the Black Street Organizations (Gangs) evolved into their own unique and distinct identity.
4. Poverty plays a contributing role in the internal dynamics of Black Street Organizations.
5. The Black Gangster mentality is a socio-psychosis. A cultural mutation that has indirectly manifested within the depths of our historical miscarriage; e.g. The Genocidal System of Slavery, Jim Crow and the Willie Lynch Methods/System. We cannot separate our present psyche (i.e. State of Mind) from our past

four hundred years or more (1619-2017) from the painful suffering we have yet to recover from.

6. The introduction of PCP in the early and mid-1970's contributed to the rapid escalation of Black Street Organization/gang violence during the 1970's.

7. The introduction of crack-cocaine in the early 1980's contributed to the rapid expansion of Black Street Organizations/Gangs, and increases in related violence, as well as increases in teenage pregnancy/promiscuity and HIV/AIDS.

8. Not all Black Street Organization members are involved in criminal activities or violence.

9. Many of our New Afrikan Youth have no sense of hope or a sense of a future; in their minds they can't even see past the age of 18, where either imprisonment or a violent death awaits them. Their Street Organization (i.e. extended family) gives them purpose, something to live or die for.

10. We are New Afrikan Activists, and we favor education, transformation, rehabilitation, prevention and vocation over imprisonment. The government pro-police approach to the Black gang problem, which truthfully has not solved this crisis, unfortunately, has only politically and economically exploited this crisis, and the mass incarceration of our young people is indicative of that exploitation.

11. Our Afrikan Amerikan (aka New Afrikan) youth deserve our love, compassion and understanding. We have failed them, and we are committed to saving them, not to destroy or give up on them.

12. It is imperative to our success we gain/earn the trust of our young gang members. Without trust they won't listen to us or participate in our programs/projects. Many of the grassroots organizations haven't had a major impact on the Black-on-Black gang violence.

> **Note**: Now, I would agree the Nation of Islam (NOI) has had one of the most influential impacts on Black Males in general, especially behind the walls, we can never take that from the Nation and the good work they continue to do – I was once a Soldier in that great Nation. I am only referring to the reality (i.e. The Truth); most New Afrikan Organizations, political, radical or religious, have failed to impede the death of our young Black Youths. One thing we have learned; the vast majority of

Black Street Organizations trust no group who works with the government or the cops. The Black Progressive Prison Rights Movement will not work with either. The Operation Hip-Hop Rescue Movement (OHHR) will work with New Afrikan grass-roots organizations and/or Activists 100% accountable to the Community, and saving the lives of our Black Children.

13. The Hip-Hop Culture/Community has the greatest potential to affect the Black Street Organizations in a positive way.

14. Our goal is not to destroy the Black Street Organizations, but to transform them, and eradicate the negative elements.
    For example:
    a. Unprincipled violence.
    b. Drug use and dealing.
    c. Unemployment.
    d. Illiteracy.
    e. No knowledge of self or heritage.
    f. Promiscuity.
    g. Teenage Pregnancy.
    h. Alcoholism.
    i. A sense of hopelessness.
    j. No sense of responsibility.
    k. No respect for the Community or our Elders.

Ages one through fourteen represent many of the different areas we have analyzed, studied, examined and re-examined. Now armed with a concrete understanding, we can develop our own method(s) and approach. The following is a functional manifestation of our method of operation, but by no means is it a solution in of itself. It is only one of the many components we intend to implement in our endeavor to stabilize our communities and chart a new future for our young people and Community.

The Hip-Hop Culture Community Center
HHCCC

The vast majority of New Afrikan Gang Members are into Rap Music and the Hip-Hop Culture. This is something most of these Black Street Organizations can relate to. Our goal is to use Hip-Hop as a medium to transform the New Afrikan gang member. Hip-Hop/Rap music will attract the gang bangers attention.

The Hip-Hop Culture Community Center (HHCCC) will not be one center, for this will not be practical or safe at the initial stages of development. Trying to get rival gangs to show up at one center at one time is too risky. We will develop multiple centers. In every community there are vacant houses and/or buildings which we will convert into a functional HHCCC. For example: Let's say we find a vacant house, three bedrooms, living room and a kitchen, each room/space will have a specific function. We will turn one room into an actual recording studio, another room into a classroom for learning about the business side of the Music/Rap Industry. This room will have computers and wall to wall shelves of books, pamphlets and other literature on business relating to the music industry. Another room will serve as the HHCCC Library of Black History.

It will contain wall to wall books on Black History written by New Afrikan/Afrikan Scholars, such as: J.A. Rogers, Marcus Garvey, George L. Jackson, David Walker, James George, Dr. NAIM Akbar, Malcolm X, Vincent Harding, Denmark Vesey, Chancellor Williams, Frances Cress-Welsing, John Herik-Clark, Cheikh Anta Diop, Haki R. Madhubuti, to name a few. The fourth room will serve as the lyrical/writing room. In this room they will learn how to write or improve their writing skills, not just rap lyrics, but also R & B. We will strategically, but inconspicuously incorporate an educational curriculum inside the HHCCC programs. We know most gang members don't like school, so it would defeat the purpose if the HHCCC resembles a school setting as most gang members would resist this approach. **The focus on Hip-Hop/Rap would facilitate our educational endeavors and the transformation of the gang members, as well as the gang themselves.**

Having the HHCCC will not attract the gang member, we will print and distribute copies of a flyer directly to the gang members/Street Organizations. This flyer will list all the benefits of participating in the HHCCC.

For example:
1. We will help them write their own songs.
2. We will record their song(s) for them.
3. We will help to promote and market their original written songs/recordings.
4. We will select the top five (5) Rappers/Rap Groups in the area and take them on a local tour around the city.

The Coordinators of Operation Hip-Hop Rescue (OHHR) will develop a working relationship with the local radio stations with Rap and Music labels, Rap Artists, Hip-Hop Magazines, Black Entertainment TV, Bounce TV, Hip-Hop Clothing Companies. We will request their support and contributions to assist us in this worthy endeavor.

Let's say gang members from a particular area fulfilled our established criteria such as:
   a. They have successfully initiated and maintain a truce with their rival(s).
   b. They have made a strong effort towards ridding their Street Organization of hardcore drug use, e.g. Crack Cocaine, PCP, Heroin, Meth/Acid.
   c. They are respecting and protecting their female members.
   d. Respecting and protecting the New Afrikan Community.
   e. Taking advantage of the educational opportunities provided by the HHCCC.

When the above criteria are achieved by certain Street Organizations, that Street Organization(s) will be eligible for:
1. We will establish with the local radio station(s) to set aside one hour a week to play songs from ten of the top performers from the Street Organization(s) that achieve all the above five(5) criteria.(Note: every week there will be a different gang top performer).
2. The top five (5) performers from this Street Organization (in addition to No. # 1) will also go on a ten city tour.
3. The top two (2) performers from this Street Organization (in addition to No.1 & 2) will be on the cover of a Hip-Hop/Rap Magazine.
4. The top performers from this Street Organization will be eligible for a state-wide lottery; He/She will be given a set of numbers; if

his/hers number is selected, they will be selected to appear on BET 106 and Park.

5. We will select the Top three (3) performers from this gang and shop their recordings to the Top Rap/Music recording labels.

Note: The above will depend on our ability to convince BET, The Radio Stations, Recording Labels and Hip-Hop/Rap Magazines to support our Movement.

The HHCCC will also sponsor a weekly Rap battle competition between rival gang members at a neutral site. Once the HHCCC's are well established in the Community, they will attract the attention of the most hardcore and influential gang members.

The Hip-Hop Dance Academy – HHDA

The HHDA will be constructed on a similar foundation as the HHCCC. They will also be Community based. The HHDA will teach all Hip-Hop Dance moves from both past and present dances, e.g. Krump/Klown, Chicken-Head, Bank-Head, Hyphing, Harlem Shake, Snap Dance, Dougie. The HHDA will also develop local dance leagues that will compete with other dance group/teams. These local teams will battle each other for a prize(s). The top local teams will compete against other top local teams from other cities in their counties. The winner of this local competition will be eligible to compete in a state competition (i.e. championship). The state champion will be eligible to compete in a national championship representing their state. The battle of champ ions can be aired on either Bounce or BET, sponsored by Oprah, Cash Money, Jay-Z, Puff Daddy, Snoop Dogg, 50 Cent, Drake, Young Money Record, Russell Simnons, XXL Magazine, to name a few. The HHDA will also have a national Hip-Hop Dance Troupe that will travel all around the country/world. The young Sistas/Brothas who participate in the HHDA will also be provided educational and vocational opportunities. We intend to use their love for dance as an educational incentive.

Note: This concept was/is inspired by Tommy the Clown: www.tommytheclown.com.

The Hip-Hop Pageant – HHP

Unfortunately, many of our young New Afrikan Sistas have low self-esteem or none. When it comes to their body image as New Afrikan/Afrikan Women, too many of our young Women have little respect for their Afrikan bodies, and fail to positively embrace their Afrikan-Features. The HHP will exist on three (3) levels: 1) Local 2) State, and 3) National. The state and local level may establish its own criteria, rules and prizes, but the national competition will be subjected to a stricter standard. Each level must celebrate BLACK BEAUTY and promote our Sistas in Hip-Hop and the role they play in the Hip-Hop Culture. <u>NOTE: NONE OF THE HHP WILL BE RUN BY A MAN ON ANY LEVEL</u>. This is a mandatory mandate. The National Hip-Hop Pageant will be more of a Cultural and political statement, challenging the Euro-Centric standards of beauty.

The following overview applies to the National HHP:
The National HHP will serve as a medium not only to promote the Hip-Hop Culture, but more important, our Natural Black Afrikan Beauty. No weaves, No Fake-Nails, No fake breasts, No fake nose, No colored contact lenses; everything MUST BE REAL AND NATURAL. The National HHP is rooted in the motto. "Keeping it real." Unfortunately, many of our young Sistas are not keeping it real. They dye their hair blond/red etc. They wear fake weaves, fake nails and colored contact lens. They get nose jobs and breast implants as well as thigh/hip and buttock reductions. Our sistas are being orientated by the popular media to despise and reject their natural Black Afrikan Beauty. Many of our Sistas view natural hair as an ugly or outdated fashion statement, a throw-back to the late 1960s. Our natural or traditional Afrikan hair-styles such as Afros, Cornrows and Dreadlocks have been designated by non-Afrikans as inappropriate for the work place. We as a People have allowed this European dominant culture to define what is natural for us as outdated or inappropriate, and like slaves we willingly submit to their warped definitions and standards of beauty which are based solely on physical features common to most European women. Our Sistas are rewarded daily for adopting what is for us an alien or non-Afrikan

standard of Beauty. The HHP national level seeks to challenge this thinking by only rewarding Sistas who keep it real, i.e. Natural. We won't reinforce self-hate and/or self-rejection. We will embrace all our Sistas of all sizes and shades if they are all natural, may they be Afro-Cuban, Afro Mexican, Afro-Puerto Rican, or a Sista from Britain, Spain, Asia or Yemen. We embrace ALL BLACK Women/Girls of Afrikan heritage. The Natural HHP is a platform for promoting Afrikan-based standards of Beauty and New Afrikan-Afrikan Artists, Fashion Designers and Hair-Stylists. We are celebrating all phases of our Afrikan Cultural Heritage.

Pageant Contestants will compete in six (6) competitions:
1.   Evening Gowns.
2.   Hip-Hop Gear.
3.   Free-Style Rap.
4.   Hip-Hop Dance.
5.   Hip-Hop Pop-Quiz: all questions will pertain to the role of Black Women in the Hip-Hop Culture and Rap-Music Industry.

Note: NO ONE PARTICIPATING IN THE HIP-HOP OPERATION RESCUE MOVEMENT WILL USE THE WORD NIGGER, BITCH OR WHORE IN THEIR LYRICS. THERE WILL BE NO SWIM-SUIT COMPETITION IN THE LOCAL, STATE OR NATIONAL HHP. THE HHP WILL NEVER BECOME A POLITICAL PLATFORM TO PROMOTE TRANSGENDER RIGHTS, EQUALITY OR POLITICAL AGENDA. THE HHP IS 100% DEDICATED TO OUR BLACK WOMEN/GIRLS, AND WE WILL NOT ACCEPT BEING HIJACKED BY OTHER INTERESTS.

We envision these prizes:
1.   Cash prize.
2.   Kilaika Shakur Scholarship.
3.   ASSATA SHAKUR BLACK WOMEN AWARD.
4.   Recording Contract.
5.   Hip-Hop Gear.
6.   A Cover shot on a Hip-Hop/Rap Magazine(s).

The young Women selected by the panel of Judges will be the face and voice of Hip-Hop, the Ambassador of Hip-Hop, travelling all over the country/world promoting the Hip-Hop Culture and real Natural Black

Afrikan Beauty. She will also appear on several TV and Radio programs. I reiterate. The National HHP will not promote euro-centric standards of Black Beauty. We will accept no Sistas with weaves, breast implants, extensions, nose jobs, blonde hair (unless it is their natural color). We will accept no Sistas who dye their hair (if you have gray hair or no hair, represent your natural God given Beauty). We will not discriminate against any Sista, may they be large, thin, dark or light. Now, the local and state HHP (though I am personally against it) can allow Sistas to participate in their HHP who wear weaves/extensions, fake nails. This change in policy on the local and state level is designed to get as many of our young Sistas involved as possible in our local and state HHP. Inviting all our Sistas would allow us to expose them to our Natural Black Beauty by preparing them for our National HHP where the contestants must ALL be natural and real, nothing fake or Eurocentric.

The Hip-Hop Amateur Athletic Association HHAAA

We have seen a direct parallel between the closure or inadequate funding of recreational facilities, programs and projects (and this includes after school programs) with the increase in adolescent violence and criminal behavior, so the role sports has played in our communities is not even a question. We can no longer afford to solely depend on local government. We must develop our own sports league. The HHAAA is designed to develop discipline in our young people, promote physical health and fitness, as well as keep our young people actively involved in positive activities.

The HHAAA will develop a league in the following sports (to name a few):
1. Mixed Martial Arts/Martial Arts.
2. Boxing.
3. Wrestling.
4. Archery.
5. Swimming.
6. Track & Field.
7. Baseball.

8. Handball.
9. Paintball Competition.

We will establish several age group leagues. We understand sports alone will not solve this crisis, but in conjunction with other community-based programs, it will play an effective purpose and supporting role.

The Original Gangsta Truce Council OGTC

The O.G.T.C. will consist of at least the two (2) of the highest ranking or most influential members of the street Organizations/Gangs in particular areas/communities. The O.G.T.C. Director, Deputy Director and Treasurer will not be gang members, but well known Community-Activists the Street Organizations trust and respect. These Activists must not be connected or associated with the Government/Law Enforcement or programs and campaigns sponsored by them. It is imperative the O.G.T.C. have the complete trust and respect of the local gangs.

The O.G.T.C. will be a non-profit association responsible for:
   A. Establishing and maintaining a truce between rival gangs in their jurisdiction.
   B. To establish and maintain a clear line of communication between the different Street Organizations/Gangs and Grassroots Organizations/Groups in their area of operations.
   C. To monitor the truce and address all issues that may or will threaten the truce and peace.
   D. To encourage their members to participate in the programs listed in this proposed draft.

The O.G.T.C. will have an office in their jurisdictions. We understand this is a 24 hour/365 days a year job – yes, a job. The O.G.T.C., including the Gang Leaders within the O.G.T.C. will be paid at minimum $15.00 an hour (8 hour work shifts), and they will earn every cent. This will be a dangerous job, even for the Gang Leaders, and it is only right and fair for them to earn a living and decent wage for their services and sacrifices, as well as the hard work required "to get the job done." The Gang Leaders within the O.G.T.C. must also remember this is a job, and if they fail to work and achieve what is listed in A-thru-D, they will be fired, and it will be up to the remaining leaders to consolidate their strength to maintain the truce and protect the integrity of the O.G.T.C. The fired individual(s) will be given every opportunity to fulfill their responsibilities; before they are fired they will be placed on notice, and then a 90 day probation period to step up his/her contribution or effort to the four (4) listed objectives, but if they fail to step up, then his/her Street Organization must elect/select another representative(s) to sit on the O.G.T.C.

    Note: The O.G.T.C. can only work if all the other programs in this proposed draft are implemented and functional, besides our Community Security Protocol Mandate.

The Hip-Hop Trust Foundation – HHTF

Every city that implements this proposed draft will be eligible to establish a Hip-Hop Trust Foundation (HHTF). The HHTF will fund "Operation Hip Hop Rescue: "A Movement"" and all programs related to the OHHR.

We envision the funds will come from the below sources:
1. Rap artists.
2. Rap/music labels.
3. Entertainers/celebrities.
4. Hip-Hop magazines.
5. Hip-Hop clothing companies.
6. Professional athletes.
7. Donors/donations.
8. Fundraising.
9. New Afrikan/Afrikan businesses.
   Note: The HHTF under no circumstances will accept any funds, grants, donations or any money from the government/law enforcement directly or indirectly.

A Petition for Institutional Restitution

Abdul Olugbala Shakur

A Petition for Institutional Restitution

Preamble

We understand Prisoners from all racial/cultural backgrounds were victimized by the California Department of Corrections' (CDCr) long term Solitary Confinement/Isolation campaign, and by no means will we ever diminish their unjust suffering, but we represent a class of New Afrikan Political Prisoners fighting this fight since the 1960's when no one else was, and they have sacrificed more to this prison struggle than anyone. Their leading roles in the Hunger Strikes and Campaign to shut down the Control Unit Prison/Security Housing Unit (SHU) (i.e. solitary confinement) is just another example of their collective effort and consistent dedication and commitment towards combatting racial oppression/persecution, plus fascism. We ask of you to understand our campaign, and the integrity of our intentions. This Petition for Institutional-Restitution is designed to bring *justice* to those New Afrikan imprisoned activists persecuted and tortured for their political beliefs and activities since the 1960's. If they don't deserve to be compensated, then who does? These Brothers have sacrificed their lives to this just cause for the last 60 years.

Support or Call for Justice

The following is what we believe to be just, fair, and reasonable requests for the inhumane treatment many New Afrikan Politically Active Prisoners were subjected to regularly while they were being held in Solitary Confinement/Isolation both at Pelican Bay and Corcoran State Prison's.

The Amerikan Judicial System strongly claims they believe in the full restoration of those who have been victimized unjustly, and being in prison does not negate the rights of Prisoners to receive restorative justice from a system that has (and continues to) commit crimes against them (us) under the manufactured cloak of combatting prison-gangs. Via the Ashker v. Government settlement the Prisoner-Class proved their case beyond a reasonable doubt; even the Judge had strongly recommended the CDCr and Government settle out-of-court.

Note: The CDCr had criminalized the political beliefs, activities, and their history of the New Afrikan Politically conscious Prisoner-class, explicitly qualifying this Class of Prisoners by international law and international standards/definition Political Prisoners/POW. This Class of Prisoners (i.e. New Afrikan Political Prisoners) were being denied release from solitary Confinement and Parole because of their political beliefs and activities, thus, becoming imprisoned because of those political beliefs and activities. Even a Judge ruled she had concerns the CDCr may have taken a race-based short-cut and assume anything concerning Afrikan-Amerikan History and Culture would be banned under the guise of being gang activities. This New Afrikan class of Political prisoners held in solitary confinement at both Pelican Bay and Corcoran State Prison was often unjustly penalized for their political activities, including their writings and reading literature. Many were also penalized for saying "Hello" to one another and given disciplinary reports for rule violations; manufactured violations to justify their continuous confinement in Isolation. This is why this Petition for Institutional Restitution is requesting restorative justice for this class of Prisoners, because it is evidently clear their persecution (i.e. Long-Term Isolation, Torture, Racial discrimination, Censorship, to name a few) was directly based on their Political beliefs/activities, and their racial and cultural background as New Afrikans.

Restorative Justice Request

1. While spending decades in Solitary Confinement/Isolation, i.e. the Security Housing Unit (SHU), this Class of New Afrikan Political Prisoners, for the most part, could not participate in several Educational/Vocational, and/or Self-Help programs, and as a result many could not obtain the criteria to become suitable for parole. These New Afrikan Prisoners who fall under this class should not be held to the same standards of the general population, especially since the CDCr illegally denied them the opportunity to obtain their

suitability by keeping them in Solitary Confinement/Isolation for decades.

2. It is Restorative Justice that the New Afrikan Political-Prisoners Class be determined suitable for parole based on the following the criteria:
    a) How much time they have served on their sentences.
    b) Family Support.
    c) A source of legitimate and legal financial support.
    d) Job opportunity if applicable.

*Those who do not meet these criteria should be entitled to be housed in a prison such as San Quentin State Prison where programs are available to will help them become suitable for parole.

3. Many of the New Afrikan Prisoners who fell under the above stated class while in Solitary Confinement received several questionable Rules Violation Reports (RVRs: Disciplinary Reports) for allegedly engaging in promoting prison-gang activities, when in fact the CDCr had reduced Black History Books/Literature to gang material and gang political activities to justify keeping them in Isolation. Many of these New Afrikan Political Prisoners received additional time in Solitary, more time in prison and denied parole because of the CDCr's illegal scheme of transforming Black History/Literature to gang-activity, which made having possession a serious rule violation.

4. The above stated New Afrikan Class of Prisoners had served 20 to 50 years in Solitary Confinement/Isolation. They were released into general population with no consideration for the damages the CDCr caused them, and then they were treated like all other Prisoners. They are not like just any other Prisoner; they are a rare and unique Class of Prisoners: They were subjected to decades of both psychological and physical torture, which includes sensory deprivation: they should have the option to serve their time in a prison like San Quentin State Prison, providing them with the opportunity to heal.

Note: We understand many Prisoners had served long-term confinement in Solitary/Isolation within the CDCr, but this Class of Prisoners was the only Class specifically targeted for their Political beliefs and activities, plus their race.

5. We are requesting a hearing before a panel made up of the following proposed individuals:
    1) Federal Magistrate.
    2) CDCr Secretary or Director.
    3) Board of Parole Hearing Commissioner.
    4) Prisoner Rights Attorney.
    5) Civil Rights Attorney.
    6) NAACP-Rep.
    7) Black Community Activist.

People, this is only a proposal, it is not set in concrete. The proposed panel should not consist entirely of government or law enforcement officials. Each New Afrikan Political Prisoner will be provided an opportunity to tell their personal experience and why they should be released/or given a parole date. This will not be required. Each affected Prisoner who represents this Class will have the option to speak to this panel. The opportunity should/must be provided; a public hearing discourages the Government from covering up Human Injustices being committed in their name.

6. This small Class of New Afrikan Political Prisoners meets both the state and federal low-risk assessment. For example:

    a) They are all above the age of 50
    b) They all have served over 30 years of imprisonment.
    c) They all have outside support.

We request their immediate release.

New Afrikan Community
Security Protocol
Mandate

WE AS A PEOPLE ARE
OBLIGATED TO SECURE OUR
COMMUNITIES AND MAKE IT
SAFE FOR OUR PEOPLE TO
LIVE IN AND PROSPER

New Afrikan Security Protocol Mandate

Mission Statement

I am a New Afrikan Revolutionary freedom fighter, who has spent the last 29yrs in solitary confinement/isolation. However, I have resisted every effort by my keepers to destroy my Revolutionary spirit. I remain active in our new Afrikan Independence Movement. If I must spend the rest of my life in prison in the service of our continuous slave revolt, so be it. I will do so in a constant state of resistance. The abduction, rape, molestation and murder of our children are becoming more frequent. Our women, may they be prostitutes or college students, are more becoming victims of abuse, serial rapists and serial killers. Our elders fear the youth in the community. Outsiders who own the local liquor stores, grocery markets, laundromats, landlords, even the police disrespect our communities. I am talking about our inability to secure our own community which simply means:

1. Protecting our children from abuse, violence, rape & molestation, abduction or abandonment.
2. Protecting our women from violence, rape & molestation, abduction, prostitution and stripping in clubs.
3. Protecting our communities from internal threats which include drugs and alcohol.
4. Protecting our Elders from abuse violence crime fraud and exploitation.
5. Protecting our communities from outside discrimination disrespect abuse and exploitation.
6. Protecting our communities from all outside threats.
7. Protecting our communities from all outside dependence.

When we speak about a secured community we are speaking about a community with the capacity to protect its members from any threats. Secured communities develop and establish their own education institutions and do not depend on the enemy government to teach our children/people. Secured communities feed their hungry, house their homeless and employ their unemployed. When I see a sista stripping to raise funds for college tuition or prostituting her body I see an unsecured community. It is also the community's responsibility to prepare New Afrikan Prisoners for release back into the community and assist them in their endeavors to readjust.

The majority of our people equate a secure community with government and law enforcement. This is our community's grave error. I understand the fear and frustration of our community, but we can't allow frustration to impair our vision to see the clear truth. Our community depends on a government that would rather incarcerate our young people instead of educate them. They would rather build new prisons than new schools. Employ more pigs to patrol and terrorize our communities instead of providing employment for our people. This government has drastically failed to secure our communities. They don't intend to. The government is more concerned with suppressing our communities and using the crime epidemic as a cover to conceal their true agenda. I ask you, despite the mass incarceration of our people, do you feel any more secure? I know the answer is "no." We must now develop and employ our own method, plan and national strategy that would simultaneously save our young people and not feed them to the prison industrial slave complex.

Article One section – A

First, we need to develop and embrace our own definition of security and a secured community. Our community has been embracing the government's interpretation of a secured community. That interpretation encompasses sending all our young BLACK MALES to prison. By occupying our communities with a bunch of racist pigs, have us snitching on each other, breeding distrust among our people, spending more money on building prisons and brutalizing our young brothas and sistas at the hands of racist and repressive pigs. (Note: These are not peace offers. There's nothing peaceful about police brutality, the gunning down of unarmed brothas and sistas or false imprisonment.) The government's definition of a secured community has brought us only pain and stress.

My beloved people, it is time for us to develop the blue print towards constructing a secured community based on the fundamental needs and concerns of our communities. I recalled when a community activist conveyed to me her community was more secure since they ran the prostitutes off from her street. This form of individualism contributes to the deterioration of our Community infrastructure.

I had explained her definition of a secured community is the government's definition, not ours. The prostitutes went to another street and some went to prison; those who didn't were back on the streets selling their bodies. This was not beneficial to the community – these sistas needed our help. How is this securing our communities? I told this sista we define our success based on how many sistas we can save from the life of prostitution and imprisonment. This is how we secure our community.

A Secured Community means:
1. Having the functional capacity and capabilities to protect our children, women and elders from violence, abuse, exploitation and harm. It also means protecting our sistas from punk-ass pimps or abusive men and husbands.
2. Having the functional ability to protect our community from any threat both internal and external.
3. Having the functional ability to educate our illiterate.
4. Having the functional ability to feed our hungry.
5. Having the functional ability to house our homeless.
6. To own and control all the businesses and homes in our community.
7. To control the flow of water and electricity in our community.
8. To police our own communities.
9. To become self-sufficient and not dependent on this government.

My beloved people, having a functional capacity means developing and establishing our own institutions that will serve our life giving and life-sustaining needs. This is the blue-print to a secured community.

Article one section-B

When I was growing up in San Diego, I can say with confidence no child was ever abducted by a child molester in our community. None of the sistas were victims of a serial rapist or serial killers. When a sista was attacked we responded. Where I lived in San Diego the 32nd Naval Base was not far from our community. The sailors had to pass through either the new Afrikan or the Mexican community to get downtown and back to the base. Most of the white sailors had the habitual propensity of propositioning every sista they came in contact with, as if all black women are potential prostitutes or an easy lay. We became fed up with this disrespect, so Haki Lumumba, a soldier in the Black Liberation Army (BLA) suggested we address this issue the next time a sista (our women and teenage girls) were disrespected. As anticipated, the disrespect for our women continued. A young sista (aka lil Girl) was dragged into a vacant house and sexually assaulted by two or three white sailors. The following day we responded, and from that day on sailors would no longer have a safe passage through our communities. The Revolutionary Men of our community responded to an issue that left our sistas vulnerable to disrespect and physical harm, and I don't regret my participation or my sacrifices. Our message was clear and the sailors eventually got our message. We believe as men it is our responsibility to create a safe living environment for our children, women and elders.

Though this was not a collectively organized program, the community culture at the time emphasized adult supervision; meaning wherever children played, there were adults in the immediate area who discouraged child molesters. There are some child molesters who get more sexually aroused when the situation is more challenging and this is why an organized and conscious effort/plan must be initiated.

When I was 13 years old, I remember my friend, lil'Nate and me hitting rocks with a baseball bat in the alley behind my house. While I was searching for rocks to hit, I looked up and noticed a yellow-green fire bird with a white guy in it talking to lil' Nate. Nate yelled and told me this guy wanted to play with us. Nate was 11 years old. He didn't understand what this guy was asking, but I knew exactly what he was suggesting. As I walked up to the car on the driver side, I swung my bat through the window hitting the sick bastard in his face.

The fact is there will be child molesters, rapists and serial killers willing to take the risk of getting caught. They often view the risk as part of the thrill and this is why it is imperative for us as a community to develop a specific plan designed to protect our children women and elders. We need to develop our own security network independent from government and law enforcement.

Article One Section-C
The key to a secured community is family, and an organized and unified community. This encompasses the incorporation of (the seven-7) Principles of our Afrikan Value System (Nguzo Saba):

    a. Umoja:unity
    b. Kujichagulia: self-determination
    c. Ujima: collective work and responsibility
    d. Ujamaa: cooperative economics
    e. Nia: purpose
    f. Kuumba: creativity
    g. Imani: Faith

Before I proceed allow me to interject this brief observation. During the celebration of Kwanzaa, our people are not applying the true interpretations of these seven (7) principles. Unfortunately, Kwanzaa has been commercialized and co-opted by a bunch of Negro Kapitalist. We don't support their bastardized interpretation. We believe in the true meaning of Kujichaqulia.

We as new Afrikans (i.e. the so-called Afrikan-Amerikan) understand the importance of culture in rebuilding our family and community. The seven principles that are misinterpreted during the month of Kwanzaa, if practiced in their genuine application, can contribute towards our liberation from the culture of materialism, greed, racism, sexism and Kapitalism. The seven principles are inherent to our Afrikan value system. I believe if we expect to emancipate our people from cultural enslavement, we must organize our family and community around our Afrikan value system. For we as a people have conformed to cultural norms contrary to our true and innate nature such as individualism. This conformity has only facilitated our deterioration. We are a social people whose basic principles are rooted in collectivism, communalism and egalitarianism. This has always been our strength, but since our forced kidnap to the shores of North Amerikka, we have been systematically stripped of our true cultural norms. An effort specifically designed to destroy us as a people, and its impact is still felt today.

When a community fails to support one another or protect one another's children, it is a community that has embraced the value system of the slave master (i.e. Cultural-kaptalism). It emphasizes individualism, selfishness, patriotic arrogance and greed; are some of the very norms contributing to our insecure communities. My people, it is not an option, we must revisit our Afrikan value system-24hrs, 7 days a week, and 365days a year. We must practice our inherent value system.

When I was young, every adult in our community was not responsible, but obligated to look out for me and all the other children/youth in the community. We all knew each other parents. We knew all the new Afrikan families in our community. As a youngster I would visit all the elders in my immediate area and interact with the younger children. This was not an aberration, but indicative of most new Afrikan communities at the time. *It takes a village to raise a child* is an Afrikan socio-cultural tradition. It is not just a slogan hijacked by Hillary Clinton to use as a book title. This is a breathing and functional force in the inherent nature of our Afrikan value system that guaranteed us a secured community.

One time our neighbor was being burglarized but my father did not call the pigs. He told me to quietly go back into the house and get his gun. He hid until the two guys came out the back door. He shot at them and made them drop everything and empty out their pockets. The message was clear. We take care of each other in our community. My mother would go down the street and get collard greens from Mrs. Cooper and go two houses down and get grapes and grape fruits from Mrs. Smith. My father would go fishing at least once a month. We had a deep freezer filled with fish and rabbits we raised and killed ourselves. My father would distribute this meat to the families and elders in the community. I even raised the rabbits and chickens, and plant the gardens for my mother. We were displaying qualities of a secured community. Those qualities were the principles of our Afrikan value system.

Approximately fifteen (15) years ago a sista wrote me and asked, "What can she do to unite her community?" I told her, she should first revisit our Afrikan Value System; you must understand our original nature before our forced adaptation to social and cultural traits foreign to our true nature. We must incorporate the seven (7) principles 365 days a year. I told her she must first make sure her and her family is practicing our value systems. You want the community to reflect the values of your family so your family must become a living example. Start with you immediate New Afrikan neighbor, explain these seven (7) principles to them and how they should be implemented. For example, her neighbor was a single mother who worked late. I told her to watch her children on those nights (for free) and the days she is at work her neighbor can watch her daughter. This exchange will unite these two families. I had also explained to her both her and her neighbor have significant back yard space. Use this space to cultivate their own source of healthy food. She can grow collar and muster greens, while her neighbor can grow pinto beans, string bean, green peas, and black eye peas. They can take this same program to other New Afrikan families throughout the community. This principle is what we call Ujamaa (i.e. collective work and responsibility).

C.U.T.F

I also provided this sista with a brief example of how she can implement the principle of Ujamaa (i.e. cooperative economics). I told her she can start with bringing five to ten New Afrikan Families within her immediate neighborhood to initiate the Community Ujamaa Trust Fund (C.U.T.F). Each of the ten families must make a monthly donation to the C.U.T.F of $5 to $20, whatever each family can afford to donate a month. There will be a three year freeze on the fund. No money can be withdrawn from this trust during this three year period. The C.U.T.F will be under the direct control of a Board of Directors, which will consist of a member from each family involved. The Board will elect a Chair person, Vice Chair, Treasurer and Secretary. No one person can withdraw from the C.U.T.F. It will take the signature of all Board members and at least two Board Members will go to the bank and the both must sign a form at the bank. The bank will be instructed to freeze the account if someone is trying to clean out the C.U.T.F account or withdraw over 30% of the account. The bank will immediately text/phone each family involved. C.U.T.F will have clear established rules which will limit the amount that can be withdrawn at one time. These are just some of the security measures designed to secure the C.U.T.F.

The C.U.T.F will be used to benefit the community:
1. To help pay the bills of those community members having difficulties paying their bills.
2. To repair broken windows, doors and heating systems/air conditioning. To repair or purchase cars for the community.
3. Family/community cook out and reunions.
4. To pay for martial art lessons for the community.
5. To legally purchase weapons to protect their community.
6. To help pay college tuition fees and establish a C.U.T.F scholarship fund, Invest in CDs stocks and bonds, mutual funds, establish an investment group and an E-Trade group
7. To help establish, build and fund community based institutions.

This was a brief example. The C.U.T.F will also help to purchase businesses inside and outside of our communities. Under no circumstances will the C.U.T.F accept funds from the government. You can even file non-profit status for the C.U.T.F, but you would have to separate number 6 & 8 and the purchasing of businesses; ventures for profit would have to be separate from for non-profit activities such as 1,2,3,4,5,7 & 9.

It is imperative you understand we are Revolutionary Nationalist, Pro-Black, Anti-Kapitalism, Anti-Imperialism, Anti Fascism, Anti-

Kolonialism, Anti-Neo-Colonialism, Anti-White Supremacy, Anti-Materialism/greed, Anti-Homophobic, nor will we promote their interest. Our goal is not to impose our beliefs on you. We will save and rebuild our communities and we believe we are ideologically equipped to do the job.

Article one section D

We must also develop our own agenda regarding dealing with gang issues. For the most part our community has embraced the government's approach, which is putting our young troubled youths in prison. This approach is motivated by fear, hate, racism and pure Amerikkkan-Fascism. These are our young people, our children, and we must approach them accordingly. We can resolve this problem without working with the "Pigs." The government's agenda is bent on destruction; our agenda is based on transformation. Transforming house street gangs into community based organizations dedicated to serving and protecting our communities.

We have no intentions of trying to destroy these street gangs. Our goal is to transform them, so our focus is to eliminate negatives such as:

1. Unprincipled violence
2. Unlicensed weapon (Note: I don't believe in disarming our communities Criminal/Gangster mentality).
3. Unemployment.
4. Selling/using drugs.
5. Drinking alcohol.
6. Promiscuity and teenage pregnancy.
7. Dropping out of schools.

This is a brief example, but we will be more successful eliminating the negatives instead of trying to eliminate the gang, which equals destroying our young people. Many have asked how this can be accomplished.

The hip-hop community/culture has the greatest influence on the vast majority of New Afrikan Street Gangs, so this will be one of the most effective tactful mediums we can/will employ to accomplish this task.

There are several misconceptions propagated by law enforcement and the mass-media/press as it pertains to New Afrikan Gangs. First , not all members in these street gangs are involved in criminal/violent activities. Each street gang has their shooters, some may just sell drugs, but each New Afrikan street Gang also has several members in college, the music industry, working an eight hour job. There are many who have never been in a police car, but these are facts law enforcement and the racist-controlled media/press never speak about because it's not in the best interest of their racist agenda.

Why is this information relevant to us as a community? It gives credence to our approach; these New Afrikan street gangs can be transformed into positive organizations. There are a handful of hard core members in each New Afrikan street gang (i.e. youth organization). We will not abandon the hard core members. We must develop a different approach for them. The government wants us to give up on them all so they can do what they want with our young people without our intervention. It's time to intervene with our youth who can be saved, and we must help them. We can no longer turn blind eyes or deaf ears to their victimization by law enforcement and government discriminatory legislations.

Article One Section-E
As I stated, it is the community's responsibility to prepare New Afrikan prisoners for release. Many of the brothas and sistas returning back to the community can either contribute to the security of our community or the insecurity of our community. This can and will be determined by their preparation and a strong outside support network.

Among all racial groups we have the highest recidivism rate, and it is obviously clear we can't afford to depend on the government or prison system. Their failure to act has only hurt our communities. Our communities have become an assembly line, producing human commodities to fuel the U.S. government prison industrial slave complex. This is why prevention and rehabilitation programs are not in their best interest. Crime and gang violence in our communities means job security for a vast majority of white males who don't care if we live or die. Our rehabilitation means their unemployment and I am determined to see them all unemployed.

My people, you have no choice but to become more active in this process. Many brothas and sistas are returning to behaviors antithetical to a secure and stable community. It is more than a word describing criminal intransigent. Failure to act only facilitates our political/and economic exploitation, plus the ongoing violence and recidivism. So emphasis must be placed on two (2) crucial aspects:

1. Prevention and rehabilitation.
2. Community based support network designed to prepare our New Afrikan prisoners for release and support them upon their release. The prison industrial slave-complex is a sanctuary designed to preserve and proliferate the criminal mentality.

This is why it is imperative for the community to become more active in the New Afrikan prisoners' rights movement. Your direct participation will guarantee your influence over matters affecting our community's security and stability.

ACT TWO SECTION –A
Preamble
This mandate is not rhetoric/propaganda; it is about concrete analysis's manifesting into concrete community based institutions. Our communities are burned out on radical rhetoric and capitalism propaganda/and or revolutionary grassroots groups refusal to work together. They want visible and substantial results. Not more words of revolution or "no peace-no justice" slogans.

People, this mandate is about stabilizing our communities and securing a future for our generations to come. We must face the fact that our children are living within dysfunctional and violent communities across this country which are producing several dysfunctional behaviors and stress disorders. We can't keep blaming racism and not accept responsibility for the role we play in our own oppression. The question I put to you all is this: what are you doing to secure our communities? Is this mandate your opportunity to contribute towards the development of our national strategy and agenda?

Article Two Section-B

We need to develop a movement solely dedicated to the development of our community without depending on, or working with the government. A stabilized and secured community will empower us with the capacity to resist any outside injustices. From economic deprivation to the dominate culture imposed misogyny. From institutionalized racism to pig brutality. We as a people cannot effectively combat external oppression/threats from a position of weakness; an insecure community is a weak community. We need a movement that will focus 100% of their time, energy, and resources towards building secured and self-sufficient communities.

The Marcus Garvey Grassroots Movement (MGGM) is what I am proposing, but it is up to every community to initiate and implement the MGGM. The following is not a complete step by step blue-print. It is a brief draft designed to provide you with a basic outline.

Step one: ORGANIZE a community meeting, inviting every New Afrikan in the community to this meeting. Provide transportation if necessary. The primary theme of this meeting will be this mandate.

Step two: ELECT/SELECT a coordinating committee. This committee will coordinate and lead the Marcus Garvey Grassroots Movement (MGGM) in their jurisdiction (i.e. city) this committee will consist of:

1. Coordinator
2. Deputy coordinator
3. Treasurer
4. Secretary
5. Program coordinator
6. Block representative
7. Information officer
8. Additional Members if needed

Step three: ESTABLISH a permanent meeting place.

Step four: IDENTIFY the needs and weaknesses of your community as well as the strengths.

Step five: DEVELOP a clear method of operation which encompasses by-laws and rules that all participants must adhere to.

Step six: We have established a set of proposals designed to address many problems plaguing our communities. You must develop methods that would facilitate the implementation of these proposals. Each proposal is the beginning stages of community based institutions. Our proposals will be distributed via our information network.

Step seven: EDUCATING and TRAINING each participant in the community to prepare them to fulfill their role and responsibility.

Note: these two (2) rules will NEVER be compromised:
1. The Marcus Garvey Grass Movement (MGGM) will NEVER work with the government or law enforcement. If we expect to be free of all oppressive constructs we cannot work with or depend on the two primary forces responsible for our oppression.
2. We will accept no government funding or grants. The government often gets control of our destiny when they control the funding. If we become dependent on the government we deserve to be slaves; the very government that would rather build new prisons than new schools. The MGGM will not accept a dime from the government. Any MGGM member/Chapter in violation of these two by-laws will be immediately EXPELLED.

ARTICLE TWO SECTION-C

We can't ignore our having a major crime and gang problem in our communities and the government/law enforcement's best response to this problem is more cops, more prisons, or more repressive laws – none of which has helped our communities. But when we lack our own national strategy we become subjugated to the dictates of others who don't love our children/youth, or have their best interest at heart.

We have no one to blame but ourselves. We threw our Youth to the damn wolves. People, this is our problem and there is no one more qualified than us to resolve the crime and gang problems in our communities. We have developed the New Afrikan Criminology Academy (NACA), which will have four (4) primary objectives:

1. To develop comprehensive literature designed to help our people understand the gang and crime problems in our communities.
2. To develop solutions to the gang and crime problems plaguing our communities.
3. To serve as a consultant advisory council instructing our communities on how to develop the community. How to develop the community based institutions specifically designed to eradicate gang violence crime and drugs from our communities.
4. To challenge the criminalization of our people and community

ARTICLE TWO SECTION-D

It is an unfortunate fact we have millions of children who are going to bed or school hungry. This is one of the saddest commentaries on the New Afrikan Community. I will not blame the government for the starvation of our children. Are we so helpless as a people we cannot feed our own children? And if the government doesn't feed our children, are they going to starve?

People, I have news for you. It is our responsibility, not the government's, to feed our children. We need to get off our irresponsible butts and feed our children. It doesn't matter if they are your biological kids or not. *It takes a village to raise a child,* and this includes feeding that child. I am not referring to those bogus celebrity Turkey handouts during the holidays. These celebrities believe they are doing something great because they pass out turkeys on thanksgiving and Xmas. If they care about feeding our children they should invest their money resources and time into community based and controlled institutions. It would provide our children three (3) decent nutritional meals a day for 365 days a year, not just only on holidays. We demand an immediate end to the exploitation of our poverty or our need for the sake of celebrity public relations.

We are developing a blue-print to construct a community based department of agriculture and food services, as well as a campaign designed to save and expand the New Afrikan (Black) farm. Hunger and starvation are solvable social crises.

ARTICLE TWO SECTION- E

Hurricane Katrina exposed our weaknesses as a people, and these weaknesses are pervasive throughout all our impoverished communities across the country. We're helpless; dependent on a government we know doesn't give a damn about us. The harsh reality is, we as men failed our community, our children, women and elders. I don't put all the blame on the government. They responded as I expected with indifference and criminal negligence. The U.S. government has neglected our communities since the first New Afrikan community was established in this country. Hurricane Katrina exposed the need for this mandate.

We are approximately seven (7) years removed from Hurricane Katrina and not one of our communities is prepared for a natural disaster, but as soon as another hurricane rips through another New African Community/city, we'll be blaming the government or racism. I am not saying this is not a valid allegation. What I am saying what is preventing you (us) from preparing our own communities? We have developed a preliminary blue print designed to prepare our communities for any potential crisis or natural disaster. It is up to us to breathe life into this blue-print. We can't blame racism for our inability to act in our own best interest. I pose this question to you all. What will be our fate if we fail to prepare our communities for the next natural disaster? That answer alone should compel us all to act.

ARTICLE TWO SECTION F

The Bunchy Carter Institute for Revolutionary Change (BCIRC) is a progressive Pro-Black (think tank) who are dedicated to transforming the New Afrikan Community into independent and self-governing communities. Hence, the first step towards our true liberation. As realists, we understand before us as a people can effectively move forward we must first stabilize our communities.

The most effective way to stabilize our communities is to approach each community as one a small country. The U.S. government has had over 400 years to prove they are both worthy and qualified to govern us and they have drastically failed. Their failure only cripples our capacity to reach our true potential as a people/community. Year after year we struggle to breathe, because we have placed our destiny and lives in the hands of a government who very survival is depend on our suffocation.

The BCIRC is still at the infant stage of our development, but we intend to resemble a provisional Government serving the needs of all our communities. Our structural formation will be similar to a government to guarantee every aspect of our needs will be address and met, but this format will also make it much easier for accountability. For example, if obesity, is a problem in a particular community or high blood pressure we can hold the community health and fitness advisor accountable obviously he/she are not doing a good job we don't want no excuses. The community will select/elect someone who is more qualified and effective. The following is only a preliminary draft:

Executive Council

    Chairperson:

    Vice Chair:

    Secretary General:

    Chief strategist:

    Chief Minister of Finance:

    Chief Minister of Justice:

    Chief of Personnel:

    National Spokesperson:

ADVISORY COUNCIL

1. Security advisor
2. Technological Advisor
3. Community reconstruction advisor
4. Education advisor
5. Agriculture Advisor
6. Intelligence Advisor
7. Gang Advisor
8. Relationship/family advisor
9. Health and fitness advisor
10. Prison Pre-release Advisor
11. Job training and job placement advisor
12. Investment advisor
13. Criminal Rehabilitation Advisor
14. Reconstruction advisor

Note: This is a preliminary draft designed to assist you in your endeavor to implement the BCIRC No. Police or government officials/politicians will not be members of the BCIRC nor will the B.C.I.R.C work with law enforcement or the government.

Each Advisor will have their own department, and each department will have its own think tank devoted to their specific area of assignment. For example: the Agriculture Advisor- her/his responsibility will be to develop a plan/program designed to eradicate hunger and starvation within the New think) tank the advisory council will be Afrika Community and the entire Black Diaspora. Every city with a significant New Afrikan population will be eligible to select/elect an Agriculture Advisor to represent all New Afrikan Communities in that city. The advisors will serve as the chair of their own department (i.e. accountable to the executive council.

The Bunchy Carter Institute for Revolutionary change (B.C.I. R.C) is solution oriented. We won't engage in senseless rhetoric/propaganda or fruitless civil disobedience. Our primary function is to solve the daily problems confronting our people. If we can't do the job, the community in that failed jurisdiction may request a new jurisdictional representative. The B.C.I.R.C. will not accept failure.

Article Two Section-G

We as a people consistently and vigorously challenge (via words) any attempt to paint us as inferior, and rightfully so, but I believe we must reinforce our challenge with our actions and deeds, and not just mere words. There's no doubt, we as a people are not genetically, nor intellectually inferior, but we have been socio-culturally indoctrinated to believe in this white supremacist mythology. The unfortunate reality is, though we challenge this myth, many of our people subconsciously live according to this myth by acting, thinking and speaking with inferiority. We see daily examples of this. One of the most profound examples is the word *nigger*. We took the power from this word by embracing and redefining its attempt to paint us as inferior, but is our justification for the use of the word really making it our own? This is one of the most dumbass statements I've ever heard. Only weak and inferior minded people would find logic in this reasoning.

Relying on our cultural and racial integrity and strength to bury that foul word is not even an option, but to surrender to its destructive influence is acceptable? This is the logic of an inferior people. No self-respecting race of people would embrace an idea specifically designed to destroy their ancestral connection, or racial identity and spirit. That we can't see this is also a symptom of an inferior complex. Another example: we live in a country we know doesn't give a damn about us, or the state of our communities, but yet we find time to senselessly murder each other at a ridiculous rate and sell dangerous drugs to each other.

Brothas neglecting, if not abandoning their children, sistas defacing their natural Black Beauty to mimic euro-centric standards of beauty; I can go on and on. These are signs of an inferior people. The most vivid example of our self-embraced inferiority is our inability to unite. We as a people have known for the past 400 years our power and strength lies in our capacity to unite and mobilize. This is the key to our freedom, but yet we can't even be one together in the face of a crisis. This is a sign of an inferior people.

One of the most significant aspects we learned from studying the Willie Lynch Syndrome (WLS) is the slave master understood if they thoroughly broke their slaves, which unequivocally encompasses the complete stripping of the slaves' racial and cultural identity and sense of self, they can (via torture, brutality, rape/molestation, murder) recreate a different people; a people orientated to self-perpetuate destructive behaviors instilled within them via the genocidal slave-system. They were right. The slave-masters viciously beat the sense of unity out of our ancestors. Even though we are hundreds of years removed from the first stage of our chattel-slavery, we still possess the unity out of our ancestors, and we have yet to restore this innate survival trait. This is an inferiority complex; psychological symptoms of a dysfunctional slave-mentality.

Note: We are well aware the Willie Lynch letter was a hoax, but its contents was/is a factual description of the methods employed by the slave masters, and it's these methods we call the Willie Lynch System. My people, I know you don't like what I am saying, but you would rather blame racism for selling drugs to our people, killing our people via gang violence, disrespecting our women and elders, using the word *nigger*, abandoning parental responsibility, trashing your own community, and pimping our Black women – this is not your fault. You are not responsible for your actions. It's all on the omnipotent white men. This is our excuse for not doing the right thing?

I reiterate, we are not genetically or intellectually inferior but we have embraced the inferiority complex. When will we learn? Are you ready to free yourself from your slave-mentality? You know, you don't need masters' permission to be free. You can stop using the word *nigger*; master won't whip your ass. Our young people say the word *nigger* is a word of endearment. What's next? Referring to our mothers as *Nappy Headed-Ho's?*

CONCLUSION

This security mandate is not a vehicle to promote neither the flawed cultural nationalist ideology of the 1960's, nor the Marxist ideology. This protocol is a mandate based on the ideological principles of the New Afrikan Revolutionary Nationalism, which is indigenous to our struggle, as slavery is to the present. It is known as New Afrikan Revolutionary Nationalism/Revolutionary New Afrikan – our struggle against Genocidal slavery: Willie Lynch Methods, Jim crow/Apartheid, Cointelpro, racism, fascism, colonialism, neo-Kolonialism, discrimination, a people on the shores of North AmeriKKKa. We need not import foreign or exotic ideologies evolved in faraway places as if we are void of our own ideological struggles. We have our own unique ideology specific to our struggle from the genocidal system of Nationalism. Our ideology evolved from Imperialism, Institutionalized racism/democratic liberalism, republican conservatism, cultural nationalism, foreign ideologies, integrationist politics, white supremacy, uncle Tommish and Kapitalism.

Our ideology has been tested, though it is still evolving, it has reached its maturity. The architects of our ideology reach as far back as pre-civil war: i.e. David Walker, Nat Turner, Denmark Vesey, Henry Highland Garnet, Gabriel and Nanny Prosser, Martin Delaney, Tunis Campbell. This is a brief example. Their contemporaries were: Queen Mother Moore, Dara Abubakari, Robert Williams, Herman Ferguson, and Imari Obadele, to name a few. Be mindful, when we speak of socialism, scientific socialism or egalitarianism/communalism, we do it from a New Afrikan perspective. These principles evolved within the vortex of our Black Liberation struggle since the organized slave-revolts.

We will not use this opportunity to impose our ideology on the people. Our priority at this stage is stabilizing our communities. I introduced this mandate as a basic blue-print to stimulate discussion about community security and development, independent from law enforcement agencies. This is not a joint project designed to cohort with local/national law enforcement agencies or government, nor will this mandate be co-opted by Negro (knee grow) organizations that work closely with government/law enforcement. This mandate is designed to ignite dialogue and mobilization. People, our freedom, our independence and empowerment will depend on the state/conditions of our communities. I ask, "What forms of pyramids are we going to leave behind? Dysfunctional communities or a united empowered and self-sufficient community under our own National flag; the red, the black and the green?" If you are serious about freedom or rebuilding our communities then help us breathe life into this mandate.

-Abdul Olugbala Shakur

New Afrikan Identity

One method employed by the slave-masters to facilitate the breaking of our ancestors was deliberately placing slaves from different tribes, villages and nations (i.e. Ewe, Ashanti, Fanti, Mashi, Dagomba, Hausa, Ibo, Wolof) on their plantations hoping to strip our ancestors of their cultural/racial identity, which includes their languages, religions and social norms. Because they spoke different languages the slave-masters believed this would prevent communication, reducing the risk of organized slave-rebellions. They also hoped to create a mindset vulnerable towards being orientated and indoctrinated into a slave thought process (i.e. slave mentality). This dynamic existed on every plantation, for it was an inherent method designed to facilitate the psychological transformation.

The architects of the genocidal system of slavery did not foresee what would happen. What they meant to destroy became our mandate from a New Afrikan perspective. Despite our ancestors on the plantations coming different tribes, villages and nations, and speaking different languages with their own social norms, they developed a means to communicate, and in doing so, it allowed them to absorb respective cultural norms. This absorption, the symbol of our ancestors, was the catalyst that brought the manifestation to a New Afrikan. I am a New Afrikan.

This is not the same Afrikan who came from Afrika. This Afrikan was indigenous to the social-political reality of the dynamics of this country.

Thus, we have the historical material – factors contributing to the basic development of our New Afrikan identity. We as a people are descendants of these New Afrikans, a representation of all of Afrika, culturally evolving in a New World. We are a symbol of our future; powerful and independent and the masters of our own destiny.

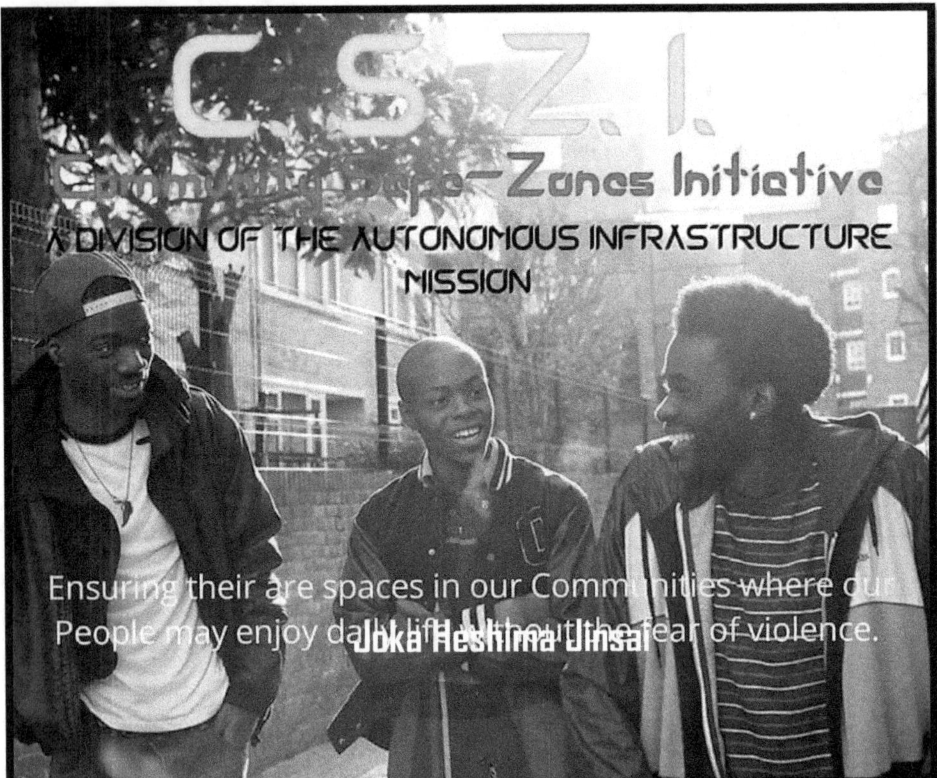

C.S.Z.I.
Community Safe-Zones Initiative
A DIVISION OF THE AUTONOMOUS INFRASTRUCTURE MISSION
Ensuring their are spaces in our Communities where our People may enjoy daily life without the fear of violence.
Joka Heshima Jinsai

The Community Safe-Zones Initiative

In underclass Communities across Amerika, and overwhelmingly in Communities of color, there are certain aspects of social life, because of our national oppression, which subject our Communities to inordinate amounts of violence. Life in the Hoods, Ghettos and Barrios of Amerika is fraught with the potential for violent death, assault or abduction, stemming from gang banging, drug trafficking or addiction, and even sexual assault. Our Elders, Women and Youth should be able to go about the daily activities of social life without fear of violent death or injury. But, because of the unique nature of our national oppression and the inescapable interconnection between subculture elements in Our Communities, and the broader Community itself, a unique solution, which does NOT rely on law enforcement and the State, is necessary.

The COMMUNITY SAFE-ZONES INITIATIVE is designed to create mutually agreed upon "safe sites" in Our Communities where Our Youth, Women and Elders can go about the daily activities of social life without the fear of violent death, assault or abduction. In every Community where sub-culture elements are organized (gang members, drug dealers, etc.), these elements also have Mothers, Grandparents, Younger siblings, Children or Little Homies and Homegirls who they love and care for, and would have no problem supporting any effort ensuring their safety.

The CSZI seeks to leverage this to identify and clearly mark specific sites in Our Communities where Our People congregate most, to establish mutually agreed upon Safe-Zones.

PROGRAM FORMAT
The Community Safe Zone Initiative will be structured into 2 major components:

1) Community Engagement Teams
2) Site Defense Teams

As with all A.I.M. Initiatives, the CSZI will employ indigenous Community Leadership as the primary elements implementing the Initiative in this Community. They will be tasked to educate the Community on the Initiative and recruit both Community Engagement Activists and Site Defense Activists; organizing them into teams to bring the Initiative to life.

COMMUNITY ENGAGEMENT TEAMS:

The CSZI Community Engagement Teams, or CET's, will comprise of members of the Community who possess good interpersonal skills and enjoy positions of relative respect by both sub-culture elements and the broader Community. O.G.s, former Homies and Homegirls who are still respected and Community Activists will explain, in detail, the purpose and intent of the CSZI. They will identify those sites and areas in the Community designated Safe-Zones, and seek to secure mutually binding agreements from sub-culture elements both in the Community, AND THOSE OPERATING IN OPPOSITION TO THOSE IN THAT COMMUNITY, to not operate in, or around Safe-Zone sites and to respect the safety of those present on those sites regardless of who they are. The CET's will ensure all such elements have the Safe-Zones Sites map developed by the Site Defense Activists, and work closely with Community members to determine which sites will be designated Safe-Zones for purposes of the Initiative. Once determined and agreed upon, Community Safe-Zone sites will be clearly marked with the CSZI icon and will be monitored by Site Defense Teams specifically tasked to ensure the safety of our People while at those sites.

SITE DEFENSE TEAMS:

Site Defense Teams will be composed of those CSZI Activists with some security, intelligence, and tactical training from the subject Community willing to volunteer their time in 2-4 hour shifts, (depending on the number of participants) to ensure the safety and security of Safe-Zone sites. The first task of SDT's is to work closely with Community members and CET's to determine which sites will be designated Safe-Zones.

Safe-Zone sites are those places in Our Communities with the greatest concentration of congregation, and frequency of visit, for its members (e.g. local stores, the laundry mat, basketball courts, some parks, places of worship, etc.).

Once determined, the SDT's will designate the site a Safe-Zone, notify the owner of the site of the designation and adhere CSZI icons at clearly visible points on the site.

SDT's will work in teams of 3:
1) An Observer called the "Eye."
2) A De-escalator called the "Voice."
3) An (ideally armed) Intervener called the "Fist."

The Eye will monitor all activity in and around the site watching for potential threats to Our People, Women, Youth and Elders be they physical threats, potential abductors, robbers, etc. The Eye will stay in constant radio communication with the Voice and the Fist. Though designated an Observer, the Eye will be trained in the event of necessity, to physically intervene to support the Fist or act in that capacity to prevent injury, abduction, or death of anyone in or around the Safe-Zone.

The Voice must ideally be someone with excellent interpersonal skills, a commanding presence, yet assertive and diplomatic. When a potential threat is detected by the Eye, the Voice is tasked to engage the subject(s) to determine if they are indeed a threat to the Safe-Zone, and if so determine to either neutralize the threatening circumstances of the subject's interactions on the site, or to request the subject leave the site. In the event the subject is deemed an imminent threat, the Voice will summon the Fist. The Voice, though primarily a first contact and de-escalation operative, will nevertheless possess the tactical acumen to support the Fist if necessary, and act to intervene to ensure the safety of our People at risk in the Safe-Zone, if necessary.

The Fist is specifically designated to physically intervene in the event of a threat to the Safe-Zone. Because of the potentially dangerous nature of such an intervention, the Fist must be highly trained to quickly subdue, neutralize or (if need arise) eliminate a threat to the lives or health of those present at the Safe-Zone. Both the Eye and the Voice are empowered to support the Fist if necessary. The Fist, ideally, will be armed with a concealed carry permit, depending on the laws in your specific State. SDT's do NOT work with law enforcement. If a subject has been deemed a threat to a designated Safe-Zone, the mandate of the SDT's is to either peacefully remove the threat from the Safe-Zone, or neutralize the threat and forcibly remove it. Circumstances will dictate the means.

Ensuring the safety and security of Our Communities is a prerequisite to our collective success, and a common sense approach if we are to ensure social life in Our Communities is of a quality worth living.

Until we win or don't lose.

– Joka Heshima Jinsai, Founder, A.I.M.

Sustainable Agricultural
Commune

How to Start a Sustainable Agricultural Commune (S.A.C.)
with the Community

The SAC is an initiative of the Amend The 13th:
Abolish Legal Slavery in Amerika Movement

Amendthe13th.org
Initiator: Joka Heshima Jinsai

- ❖ We organize a team and we will start by canvassing and spreading the word in communities, explaining the benefits of sustainability, healthy food, building and sustaining our communities, our environment, and our health.
- ❖ We intend to find a plot, no matter how large or small, which is available to be used for communal goals.
- ❖ We link with local underclass community organizers and pool their assets, expertise and labor to educate, organize and mobilize the community's residents for the Sustainable Agricultural Commune.
- ❖ We determine which fruits, vegetables, herbs and grains are most widely consumed, popular and commercially valued in that community and area.
- ❖ Once done this must be compared to which crops among those will grow most effectively and profusely in that unique climate and environment.
- ❖ Equally essential: organizing, training, helping movement activists, community organizers and residents into the divisions of labor necessary to initiate the commune.
- ❖ We will follow the collective ownership format.
- ❖ Everyone who contributes something to that cycle will be given a commune membership card entitling them to a percentage in produce and dividends.

For more background information please visit:
SustainableAgriculturalCommune.org
Email: Sustainableagriculturalcommune@gmail.com
Twitter: @SustAgriCom
Facebook: Sustainableagriculturalcommune

NEW AFRIKAN MATH & SCIENCE CENTERS INITIATIVE
THE APPLICATION OF SCIENCE AND ENGINEERING IN OUR COMMUNITIES MUST BE PRACTICAL AND GEARED TOWARDS SOLVING THE PROBLEMS WE FACE EVERY DAY, FROM FIXING OUR CARS WHEN THEY BREAK DOWN TO PREPARING OUR OWN MEDICATIONS.
A DIVISION OF THE AUTONOMOUS INFRASTRUCTURE MISSION

New Afrikan Math & Science Center Initiative

Preamble

There is no more vital component of New Afrikan National Development than the development of our math and science capacity. Our continuing struggle to forge strong and highly developed New Afrikan Communities has been, and will continue to be, affected by applications and advances in math and science.

The impact of math and science on the progress (or retardation) of our communities' development has both an objective and subjective component that must be explored to truly appreciate its importance to our success. The gross disparities in math and science achievement between new Afrikans and those in other communities, whether by direct correlation, or mere causal association, tends to reflect the disparities in economic, educational and socio-political development at the heart of our national oppression.

This was not always the case. There was a time in human history when Afrikan Civilization was the well-spring of math and science from which all of humanity drank. The system of global white supremacy, the entire global capitalist construct itself, came into being as a direct result of scientific innovation. It will be through scientific innovation the seeds of our genuine freedom and ultimately that of the world will be sown.

With our current level of knowledge, humanity possesses the mathematical acumen, scientific knowhow and technological capacity to produce sufficient food, clean water and medicine to sustain the entire global population; to meet its energy, housing, telecommunications and educational needs sustainably. Yet we do *not*, and as a result, our communities suffer. We have yet to realize the broad-based cooperation and economic worldview to establish such an equalitarian reality because the subjective interests of world capitalism and global white supremacy have precluded it. Because of the historic oppression and generational poverty of New Afrikans across the diaspora, and here in the U.S. in particular, this state of affairs impacts our communities disproportionately. Our continued failure to adequately develop our math and science to a level comparable to our oppressors only perpetuates this state of affairs.

Throughout New Afrikan Communities in the U.S. alone, thousands of tons of food are thrown away annually rather than collected and distributed to the hungry. Millions of units of housing sit empty and remain so, rather than allow our homeless to enjoy temporary housing. Humanity possesses the scientific know-how to send spacecraft beyond the borders of our solar system (the Titan probe, etc.) and continues to receive radio telemetry from them. Humanity knows how to create and contain anti-matter, the very stuff of creation itself (the Large Hadron Collider, etc.), yet we cannot seem to muster enough math & science to build the basic infrastructure in our communities to feed, clothe, house, heal and defend ourselves. In the face of the gross and growing disparities between the haves and the have-nots, between greed and giving, between waste and wanting, we must acknowledge this system has mismanaged – woefully and criminally mismanaged – the nature and structure of human civilization on our planet. We must recognize they are *destroying it*, and have used Math & Science as the primary tools to do so.

Cultivating our Math & Science could imbue us with the capacity to meet our basic needs, reverse our underdevelopment, realize our national liberation and pave the way for a new, more equalitarian world for everyone. We cannot continue to blame systems of oppression for the retardation of our communities' development when the means to reverse it – the knowledge to forge our own infrastructure, rooted in Math & Science – is readily available to us.

If we are serious about ending the national oppression of New Afrikan People (and all People), we must apply ourselves to mastering the processes which govern the modern world. This means we must develop a basic, intermediary and advanced curriculum in four major areas, and how they can be adapted to serve our communities:

1) Foundational Math & Science
2) Computers, Technology & Electronics
3) Bio-Life Sciences
4) Structural Science and Innovation

We cannot hope to develop our communities, or sustain them in good order, without harnessing the tools of Math & Science and applying them to the challenges which define our underdevelopment in new and imaginative ways. Our approach to research and development, our employment of the very scientific method itself, must correspond to our communities' basic needs and our long-term aims. By developing our Math & Science capability, we will be better equipped to feed, heal and house those in our communities while developing new innovations to maximize the productive capacity and efficiency at providing goods and services for our people in the context of Collective Work and Responsibility (Ujima).

But doing so will be a process. The unfortunate truth is many of our youth disdain Math & Science for sports, music and dance – while many of our adults are busy with work. Many of us write and create beautiful works of art, but few show a genuine enthusiasm for Math & Science. We can change that by placing the means to develop our own autonomous Math & Science Centers in our Communities.

NEW AFRIKAN MATH & SCIENCE CENTERS

INITIATIVE FORMAT

Developing our New Afrikan Math & Science Centers (or NAMS Centers) is a process that will begin with **instructor selection and recruitment.** To carry this process out **NAMS Center Activists** will need to be recruited from the Community where the Center will be established. People who are trusted, articulate and influential, capable of articulating both the need for and vision of the NAMS Centers Initiative to their neighbors.

It will be the responsibility of these NAMS Center Activists to canvas local University and College campuses for those 3rd and 4th year New

Afrikan students, graduate students, or Professors who concur with the aims of the Initiative and who will donate their time and expertise to serve as instructors in that Community's NAMS Center. These NAMS Center Activists and Volunteer Instructors will serve as the backbone of the initiative.

NAMS CENTER CURRICULUM

The New Afrikan Math & Science Center Initiative curriculum will be divided into 4 major sub centers within the institution, offering these fields of study:

1. FOUNDATIONAL MATH & SCIENCE:

The Foundational Math & Science Department will focus on the basic knowledge which acts as the foundation for all real world Math & Science applications. All fields of study designated **Category 1 (CAT-1)** will be offered under the Foundational Math & Science Department in an incremental curriculum, where knowledge builds upon acquired knowledge.

Fields of study in CAT-1 will include:
- Basic Mathematics
- Chemistry
- Engineering
- Trigonometry/Calculus
- Biology
- Algebra/Geometry
- Economics/Finance
- Earth sciences
- Physics
- Geology

2. COMPUTERS, TECHNOLOGY AND ELECTRONICS:

The Computers, Technology end Electronics Department (or CTE Department) will focus on providing knowledge on computers, computer hardware & software, computer-assisted technology, electronics and the real world applications of these sciences to solving problems in the Community. All fields of study designated **Category 2**

(CAT-2) will be offered in this Department in an incremental curriculum where knowledge builds upon acquired knowledge. Fields of study in CAT-2 will include:

- Electrical Engineering
- Energy Technologies & Solutions
- Telecommunications Technology
- Computer Engineering/Coding
- Drone Technology
- Robotics

3. BIO-LIFE SCIENCES:

The Bio-Life Sciences Department will focus on providing knowledge in those sciences which sustain life, extend life, save life or improve life for our Communities. All fields of study designated **Category 3 (CAT-3)** will be offered under this Department in an incremental curriculum where knowledge builds upon acquired knowledge. Fields of study in CAT-3 will include:

- Bio-Medical Sciences
- Chemical Engineering
- Genetics/Cellular Biology
- Agricultural Sciences
- Pharmaceuticals
- Psychology/Psychiatry

4. STRUCTURAL SCIENCE AND INNOVATION:

The Structural Science & Innovation department will focus on knowledge which instructs us how to design, engineer, build, repair, fabricate and produce the things necessary for our communities to function and thrive. All fields of study designated Category 4 (CAT-4) will be offered under this Department in an incremental curriculum where knowledge builds upon acquired knowledge. Fields of study in CAT-4 will include:

- Architecture/Carpentry
- Manufacturing/Production
- Metallurgy
- Recycling/Reuse Technologies

- Automotive Engineering
- Energy Systems & Alternatives
- Structural Engineering
- Fabrication Sciences
- Thermodynamics
- Aerodynamics & Aircraft
- Hydraulic Sciences

NAMS Instructors will be assigned to 1 or more Departments of the Center based on their knowledge, available time and field(s) of expertise.

COMMUNITY CLASS SITES

To establish the initial physical facilities, or **Community Class Sites (CCS)**, of the New Afrikan Math & Science Centers, NAMS Activists will canvas the community, explaining the need & intent of the initiative, seeking serious and supportive Community members and institutions willing to host a CCS. CCS Hosts willing to offer the use of space (or unused properties) in homes, Churches, apartments, Mosques, basements, Temples, garages, Community Centers or anywhere working space can be provided to the Center, will make up the core of the **NAMS Community Council**, in conjunction with NAMS Coordinators, Activists and Instructors.

Once all space is identified, NAMS Coordinators, Activists, Instructors and Property Owners will convene the Council and determine which spaces will house which Departments, and at what time(s) those CCS's will be available for Center use. This will ensure Participants and Community members are aware of the specific CCS locations and class times for each Department.

FUNDING

Our Departments will require books, supplies, equipment, software and computers to teach these courses. Therefore, one of the primary functions of NAMS coordinators and Activists will be to solicit donations, contributions and sponsorships, while organizing fundraising events that further engage the community.

Those NAMS Activists with knowledge and proficiency in grant writing will be tasked to pursue grants for each eligible Department of the NAMS Center. Crowdfunding and online donation drives will be held to further fund each individual department of the Center.

COMMUNITY PARTICIPATION AND PURPOSE

Central to the success of this institution is Community participation - especially among our youth. For this reason, NAMS Activists and Community supporters, those who live right there in the hood, must make weekly education and recruiting rounds in the Community to educate our People to the importance of Math & Science to New Afrikan Communities, and taking every opportunity to recruit participants to attend the Center.

Attendance in the NAMS Center is **free** to all participants in the Community. We will accept no money from the state, nor will the NAMS Center Initiative become reliant on, or beholden to them. Success for the New Afrikan Math &Science Center Initiative must affirm our Communities self-reliance if it is to realize its aim.

As indigenous Community members become proficient in various Math & Science disciplines from the NAMS Center they will assume the formal role of Instructors Aide(s). Once an Instructors Aide has mastered both their particular field of study and the ability to teach it, She or He can assume the role of NAMS Instructor in that Department themselves. Each participant must complete the full Foundational Math & Science Department curriculum before moving into one or more of the other Departments. Though the NAMS Center Initiative intends to have participants go through each Department of the Center, we want to encourage specialization.

The primary function of the New Afrikan Math & Science Center Initiative is to equip the Community with the knowledge and expertise to build and maintain its own Autonomous Infrastructure. This means participants   must   be   strengthened   and   fitted   with   specific responsibilities within the context of the Community's infrastructural needs and a willingness to maintain those responsibilities. Once these skill-sets are developed and organized, we can move to meet the Community's needs in a comprehensive and systematic manner.

CONCLUSION

In the final analysis, it has been, and continues to be, advancements in Math & Science which contribute to the systems of oppression responsible for our Communities' instability, and dialectically it will be through our mastery of Math & Science this yoke is forever lifted. Our commitment to this course will ensure a new era of Freed0m, Justice, Equality and Prosperity is ushered in for our New Afrikan communities, and for all humanity. Think on these things, they are cause for great meditation.

The New Afrikan Math & Science Centers Initiative is a division of the Autonomous Infrastructure Mission of the Amend The 13th Movement
Joka Heshima Jinsai
Founder, NAMS Centers Initiative
Contact us for more information or to join our efforts:
Email: Amendthe13th@gmail.com
Twitter: @Amendthe13th
Facebook: Facebook.com/AmendThe13th
Web: Amendthe13th.org/math-and-science-centers-initiative

Youth Community Action Program: Part of the Autonomous Infrastructure Mission of the Amend the 13th Movement

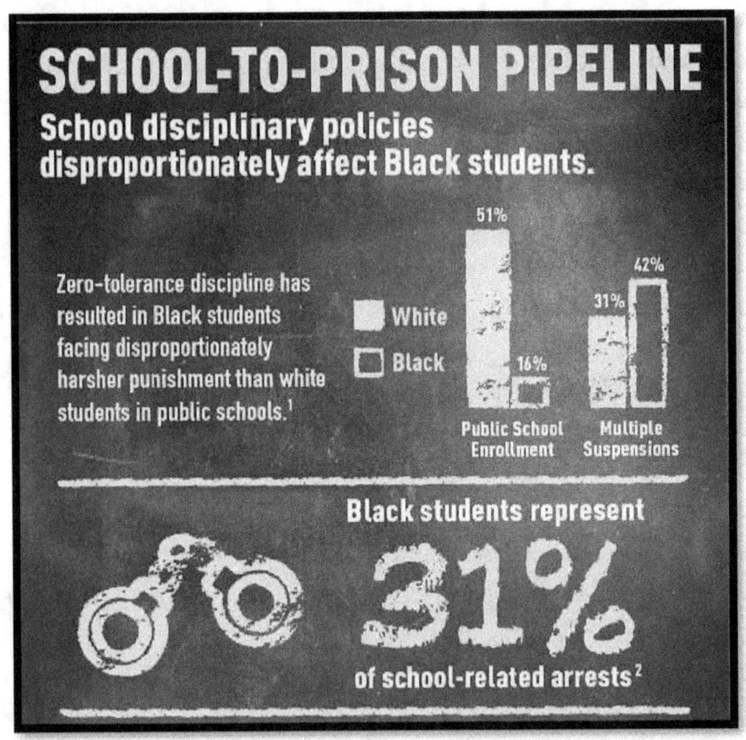

Youth Community Action Program

We propose the adoption and implementation of the Youth Community Action Program as a model for both developing and empowering our young sisters and brothers in the hoods, projects, barrios, rural towns, suburbs and trailer parks where our communities are situated. The Youth Community Action Program (YCAP) is both an educational/training program and a co-operative economic nonprofit initiative which targets underclass youth and neighborhoods employing volunteers from the youth's own community and family to work in concert with YCAP activists in a two phase development initiative.

Phase I - Involves an after school, five times a week, 2-½ hour educational and training initiative focusing on history from a true perspective (Zinn, Diop, and DelaValle) cultural awareness to retard racial conflicts and strife between oppressed nationalities and citizens stemming from stereotypes and misconceptions of Asian, New Afrikan, Mexican/Latino, Euro-American, and Middle Eastern (etc.) cultures; computer and technological literacy, the arts (visual, music, dance, etc.) and science/engineering. Three out of every five days a week the final hour will be devoted to martial arts, self-defense training and strategic thought (to promote self-discipline and critical thinking). Participants must comply with participation in Phase I to be eligible for Phase II inclusion.

Phase II - Involves establishing a collectively-owned community-based venture in which each youth participant will own an equal stake in, and be trained in, the venture which best suits them. All will receive equal revenue portions/pay (collective work and responsibility, equalitarian distribution of wealth).

Example:

Perhaps one of the more enjoyable commonalities shared by many cultural groups is a fondness for the "custom-car cultures." Building on the intra-cultural commonality, this pilot venture can be a custom-car garage (think "pimp my ride") where we can seek in-kind donations of equipment and old cars (all tax-deductible), cash donations and fundraiser revenues to fund the rest. Volunteers from this industry will train such youngsters in exchange for marketing publicity for their own ventures while we also seek industry-related sponsors. The cars will be retrofitted, rebuilt and "pimped out" into custom low riders, donks, and euro-tuners, and then put on the lot for sale and website auction. The proceeds from each sale or client "fix-up" will be split equally among the youth (50% of the profit), 20% will go to expand the nonprofit initiative, 20% will go to a college fund for them all, and 10% will flow back into expanding the venture. We, in this manner, provide them with an economic incentive to be indoctrinated into collective practices and progressive activism, bring the community closer to one another, and introduce a new source of revenue into the underclass community where that chapter of YCAP is based.

The positive social impact on our communities for our people who live in these communities should be significant.

A BLUE-PRINT TOWARDS BUILDING
SELF-SUFFICIENT COMMUNITIES
TOWARDS BUILDING A NEW AFRIKAN
-NATION-
Abdul Olugbala Shakur
Joka Heshima Jinsai

Abdul Olugbala Shakur
Freedom Campaign
6748 Mission St
P.O.Box 246
Daly City,Ca 94014
gwendolynlive@gmail.com
COMRADE ABDUL SHAKUR HAVE SPENT
OVER 40 YEARS IN PRISON AND 32 PLUS
YEARS IN SOLITARY CONFINEMENT.
HE IS BEING DENIED FOR HIS POLITICAL
BELIEFS AND ACTIVITIES,HE CONTINUE
TO FIGHT FOR HIS PEOPLE
♥♥♥